SHIMMERS OF LIGHT

SHIMMERS
OF LIGHT

SHIMMERS OF LIGHT

NEW AND SELECTED POEMS

ROBERT CURRIE

Introduction by Lorna Crozier
Afterword by Mark Abley

Thistledown Press

Thistledown Press Ltd.
P.O. Box 30105 Westview
Saskatoon, SK S7L 7M6
www.thistledownpress.com

Library and Archives Canada Cataloguing in Publication

Title: Shimmers of light : new and selected poems / Robert Currie.
Other titles: Poems. Selections
Names: Currie, Robert, 1937- author.
Identifiers: Canadiana 20220141568 | ISBN 9781771872188 (softcover)
Classification: LCC PS8555.U7 A6 2022 | DDC C811/.54—dc23

Cover and book design by Marijke Friesen
Cover image: Shutterstock
Printed and bound in Canada

Thistledown Press gratefully acknowledges the financial assistance of
The Canada Council for the Arts, SK Arts, and the Government of Canada
for its publishing program.

"Poetry is a response to the daily necessity
of getting the world right."
—Wallace Stevens

"Writing, and reading, are reasons to get up in the
morning. I can't remember the last time I was bored."
—Karen Solie

This book is for Geoffrey Ursell (1943–2021)
and for Dave Margoshes, two fine writers
who have given so much of their energies
to support other writers.

CONTENTS

YARROW

LEARNING ON THE JOB

KLONDIKE FEVER

RUNNING IN DARKNESS

WITNESS

THE DAYS RUN AWAY

ONE-WAY TICKET

NEW POEMS

INTRODUCTION
The Marvellous Moments Of Robert Currie

by Lorna Crozier

I have many reasons to be grateful to Robert Currie. He was, in my early years of writing in the mid 1970s, a mentor, first of all because of his poetry, unapologetically set in a city as obscure and off-centre as the one I grew up in, his Moose Jaw, my Swift Current. He dared, fifty years ago, when many thought that writers came from somewhere else—Paris, London, New York, perhaps Toronto—to set his poems on the streets where he grew up, fashioning small narratives from his childhood friends, his parents, the games played in back alleys, near railroad tracks, and in "the chill of Moose Jaw creek." He dared to turn the middle of nowhere, as those from away often perceived it, into the centre of the universe.

His Beatrice, his dark lady of the sonnets, is a girl from Maidstone and the site of their romantic tryst is the Capitol Theatre on Second Avenue where "the giant screen gave them somewhere to look / while their hands discovered each other." His poet's walk, described in an early poem of that title, is located not in the Lake District, the inspiring Catskill mountains, or the farmlands of Frost's New England but "beyond the asphalt / where the spruce looks darkly down," and "the sunlight seldom touches."

Not only does he position his poems in the local, but he finds a way to rhapsodize the prairies without ignoring its starkness, its closeness to elemental things, and the long, long months of cold. In one of the final poems in this collection, "Night on the Prairie," the moon is not a lantern for lovers but "a splinter of ice, / its frigid light shining on miles and miles / of empty land." Though a boy can lie on a summer afternoon "in uncut grass / with half a rhubarb pie inside / ... his skin warm alive / in blowing grass," in another poem, the breeze has picked up speed; it's become a wind, "whirling over 500 miles / of uncharted prairie moaning / across the cracked steer skull / wedged into a badger hole."

As in those images, from the first page to the last, intimations of mortality unsettle any possible retreat into complacency. In Yarrow, the mother of the eponymous hero sees the beams of the new barn rising "like bones / white in the twilight," while the speaker of the dramatic monologue, "From the Cold," describes the temperature as "cold like January maggots." Currie carries these shivers and warnings into family life. In "Closing Time," one of my favourites because of its perfect melding of love and terror, as a man with his young son locks up the cabin, he's confronted with "winter crouched beneath the beds" while "floorboards shift like thin ice underfoot."

Along with Currie's deft, unsentimental evocation of the place I love, other reasons have kept his books on my shelves through many moves and cullings. From the moment I met him and his writing I couldn't help but fall under the spell of his passionate commitment to poetry, something he kept alive even through the arduous hours of teaching high school English, a demanding job we once had in common. Though few poems in this collection bespeak the drama occurring "between the blackboard / and rows of cluttered desks," I can't help but feel that the continued presence of young people in Bob's working days inspired the many poems that chronicle childhood and adolescence. One of his strengths is his impeccable rendering of the loss of innocence and those crucial moments in life when a boy understands the world of men. Like the prairies itself, that world teems with tenderness and violence. They come together perfectly in "Father and Son: Rite": a father's longed-for touch is not a stroke on the cheek or a hug but a nightly after-supper arm wrestle that the boy longs for twenty years after.

Many of Bob's poems work like small exquisite time machines, pulling the past into the present or revealing the shadow the future casts over the singular bright moment crystallized on the page. So many times this happens but never better than in "The Volleyball Players" and "He Loved to Hear Her Play." In the former, the speaker with other adults in the stands watches the boys "who practice long hours / after school when the gym is free." Captured by their eagerness and passion for the game, the speaker claims that the hearts of the older spectators reside in the younger players and "sing again in our chests ... // We learned from you what we knew before: / to value the instant that lifts the heart and holds / us here in the marvellous moment that is now." The adult speaker of "He Loved to Hear Her Play" pictures his mother running her fingers over "black and white ivory keys

[that] remain invisible / as they would be if they were here in darkness." Relatives not seen in ages, grandparents, aunts and uncles appear, "all of them / in pairs tonight, swaying to the rhythm / of the tune my mother plays my father, / a melody he may not hear again for years." Time's divisions, past, present and future, come together in that gorgeous concluding line. And just before that happens, I am captivated by the diction of "my mother plays my father." She plays him as woman would a man in a loving flirtation; she plays him into existence in the resurrective moment of the poem.

His poems have many such moments that reclaim the lost, perhaps none more moving than the ones about Gary Hyland, a friend we shared. When I said at the start of my introduction that Bob was my mentor, I should have said that Gary was too. It was hard in those heady days of Saskatchewan poetry to think of one of them without thinking of the other. Most people will know that Gary died of ALS and that towards the end of his life, though he couldn't speak or type, he still wanted to write poems. I can think of no better tribute to him and no more moving paean to the meaning and longevity of friendship, than one of the later poems in this collection, "At Work." Male tenderness was predicated by earlier poems about other friends, including one the poet met in high school. By the time we get to the homages to Gary we're ready for them. We're ready to revel in the specialness of their bond and their fealty and love of poetry and of each other.

Almost five decades ago, both Bob and Gary—when we'd meet monthly to talk about poems with several other friends in Moose Jaw—gave me lists of books I should read. One day Bob said, "You should read Patrick Lane's *Beware the Months of Fire.* You'll love him." Bob, of course, meant I'd love his poems and I did, but those words on the page led me to the man I'd live with for forty years. Bob's poetic matchmaking is among the things I am grateful for when I enter again the generous, prairie-centric world of his poems, including the new ones in this collection, and when I revisit his poignant charting of the losses we must carry as we try, with the help of his words, to savour "the marvellous moment that is now."

THE CHAPBOOKS
(1970, 1973, 1975)

POET'S WALK

Few venture here
beyond the asphalt
where the spruce look darkly down.
>   Some stroll as far as the brook
>   that shivers over rocks
>   cold as chipped ice
>   but their eyes run with the current
>   down to the lazy lull of lake water.
They will not linger
where the sunlight seldom touches.

They shudder
if they notice
how the leaves shift into shadow.
>   It's the odd one only
>   who penetrates the underbrush
>   and discovers
>   at dusk   raspberries
bright as blood upon the brambles
as the blackness shoulders in.

FAME

Home from work, I discover
the bundle from Delta Publishing,
eager to christen my offspring,
child coaxed from printing press womb,
not spewed from my cranky old mimeo,
when my wife passes me, going out the door.
Heedless, I rip brown paper in a frenzy of excelsior.
"I've got to get downtown before six.
Your son needs his pants changed."

Reluctantly flipping him diaper free
I find a surly red butt
looking as if it had sat
in burnt scalloped potatoes,
and my three year old colour commentator announces,
"Ryan's got poop. He stinks."

Fingers that would caress
crisp pages of my poems
now wring the neck of a filthy diaper
and, hunched over the toilet bowl,
I ponder on that student today
who couldn't grasp the meaning of irony.

CALGARY NIGHT

Evening settles in.
Sitting on lawn chairs
beneath the hulk of a Calgary apartment block
we talk together for the first time in years,
content to rally memories back and forth
of the bright times when we blazed with youth.
Tonight the Bow River churns in the distance,
your old hound curls at our feet,
snorting occasionally in dreams, maybe, of distant hunts.
Against the sky the river bank mounts darkly and shadows
    drop.
The brightest thing between us and that black hill
is the sign of a Chinese restaurant
which flashes imprecations at the night.
The air, so lately drenched with summer heat,
is suddenly chilled by motorcycles
shotgunning an intersection.
Our lawn chairs shiver with the sound.
Then the blast of warring Harleys is echoed
by a kid peddling a bike, a cardboard
clothes-pinned to hammer at his spokes.
Rocked from reminiscence now, we watch him
as he wheels around the empty lot
pumping hard, picking up speed,
circling ever closer to a mound of dirt
till he's ready for the ramp
and hits it   takes off
over the Bow River, rising above its blackened bank,
soaring till the stars spray his handlebars.

TRUTHS

Looking at the photographs   I'm shocked.
We were in the castle hall with Claudius posturing,
the very torches guttering at his blustering words.
Then   Osric danced below his plumes
            and the duel was on.
Hamlet and Laertes caught in a faithless match,
fencing till the sweat ran, the cheers rang,
and Gertrude's eyes stuck on the poisoned cup.
No one was jarred by the flashbulb's pop.
There are no anachronisms in Elsinore
when Hamlet tears at Claudius's throat
and makes him toast union with death.
Yet all the photos show
is Don and Dallas, Paddy, Bob and Kathy,
kids in V-necks and blue jeans,
caught in fluorescent glare
between the blackboard
and rows of cluttered desks.
There must be a finer truth,
the one that we recall.

JOHN'S POEM

His father with a hard eye for the women,
his mother dead in an exhaust choked car,
the coroner   at least   thought of the kids,
labelled it an accident.
But it was no accident
that John strayed.
In grade nine ranked with the wilder seniors
quit football to work after school
needing money for the beer and the girls.

Strange to see him in grade twelve
practising to pantomime a scene from *Hamlet*.
No mere dumb show to him.
"Awright you guys, we gotta do this right.
Anybody laughs is gonna get it."
More than threats stilled the snickers.
John knew what Shakespeare was hitting at
and we could recognize that much.
                    After the Olivier film
one girl said what more were thinking.
"You know that closet scene with Ophelia?
Well, I thought John and Gaye did it better."
Little enough reward   I guess
for having to live a part.

INTIMATIONS

Striving to make them sense
their own mortality
I gripped the shrunken head,
a rubber toy but grisly,
addressed it as Yorick,
and no gorge rose.
But after class
one boy shied towards me:
"I was just wonderin' if ... well ...
Howdja like a real skull for that part?"
Trying not to think
of what was left headless
I seized upon his offer.
Now when Hamlet holds
the jester's skull,
the classroom grows
quiet as the grave.
They see the end
and cannot laugh at that.

CLAUDE

His voice was hardly the movement of lips
his arms skin slack on bone
but his hands remained huge
clawed at his sides
trying to tear out the growth.

Watching   I thought of Hamlet.
Not that Claude would remember him
and his tortuous efforts
to learn the readiness is all.
He'd worked on the same lesson though
walked alone under the sentence
till he could bear the load,
let people think the doctors had got it
till the truth spread along his throat.

Then   caged in a terminal bed
he sent home plastic straws   toys for the kids,
joked to wipe the worry from visitors' faces,
told his wife to ready their room for his return,
—recognized the need for pretence.
He wasn't ready to die
but he knew how a man
must go about it.

MY POEMS ARE

My poems
are slim bombs
craving explosion.
their fuses lie
dark on the page
awaiting your arrival
        with a light.

THE EYES OF MAY

The sidewalks coloured with people
and Ryan perched on my knee
for the Kinsmen Band Festival.
His big eyes paraded the street
looking for clowns with balloons
till a cannon cracked in his head
—the flypass of jets from the air base.
Eyes rolled whitely, screams spilling like tears.
And I hadn't thought of a three-year-old's fright.
For a half hour after, he shook,
with hands clamped to his head.

At home, he flips his library book,
grinning at pictures of pilots and planes,
but   streaks for the back door,
moaning, hands beating at ears
to knock away a jet's distant wail.
This morning, he edges out the door,
surveys a blue sky soaked in sunshine,
circles the yard   warily,
then bounds to his mother's side:
Nice day, Mom! No airplanes! No jet planes!
His eyes are the shining frame
for a sky that is safe.

A DAY NO PIGS WOULD DIE

Instead
the man who killed them
dead
and his son finding him
in the barn where he'd exiled himself
because of the cough that wrenched their nights.
The boy was thirteen years old
but his father
who killed for a living
had taught him of life and death
so that
he made the arrangements
did the chores
and before sundown
the clods of dirt
had turned the wooden box
into a drum echoing briefly
thought silent woods.
And then there was
nothing to do
but walk away
from the mound of fresh earth.

    Closing the book
I hear Gwen asking
    How was It?
and mumbling *Okay*
I leave the room

so she won't see
the tears that well
for a gentle man
whose job was killing pigs
and for a father
I will one day
lower to the earth
and for me
with my kids
looking down.

DIVING INTO FIRE
(1977)

RITE

They took the new boy down the tracks
to where the trestle began.
Forced to his knees
he felt like someone
bent before the guillotine
he'd seen in his grade-six reader.
But they only wanted his ear on the track
to pick up the faint hum
that soon would grow along the rails.
Wrenched upright
he swayed before the trestle
while they made a pile of rocks.
    "Ya move an we'll bury ya with em."
His eyes now were on the dot
that rose between the rails.
When he stirred ahead
a hand fell on his shoulder.
    "Not yet. We'll tell ya when."
He glanced back at clenched hands
and eyes hard as stone.
The train was black on the trestle
when they pushed him forward.
He stumbled and turned
but rocks slashing around him
spilled him ahead.
From the dark cabin
the engineer's hand
flared like lightning

and thunder rolled toward him.
His heartbeat was lost
in the toll of the wheels
as he lunged for the platform
hugging himself to the rusted barrel
that shook at the miss
and the cars shaking beside him.
When the rattle had died
without and within
he still clung to the barrel
not knowing
if he could make it back.
Nor if he wanted to.

LARGO

Behind me is the bridge
I cannot walk across.
On the far bank
a boy is crouching
sunlight bouncing
by his shadow
the bow of lemonwood
taut beneath his hand
his eye upon a gopher
peering from its burrow.
He has no thought of me
in the distance of this island.

I watch him while I can
and when I turn away
it is to cross another bridge
stretching over waters
leading somewhere out of vision.
No way leads back to him
or even here again.

THE DIVER

The bridge like a Roman fort
held the river and the beach,
held our vision steady through waving heat,
held us all while the solitary figure
struggled up the arch,
his knees braced against the rivets.
Below someone shook out his towel
while others bet upon his chance.
At the summit of the span he rose,
his arms outstretched
flung a cross against the sun
and the whole world hung beneath him,
our eyes nailing him to the sky.
Suspension for an instant and forever.
A slow plunge toward the water
and he came down from above
dropping beneath the surface like a stone.
The river circling away
grew silent as held breath
                    still as death.
Then from unknown depths
his head broke the water,
shook out a crown of sunlit spray,
brought release   new life
thrilling in our chests.

NOW THAT SPRING IS HERE

The last Sunday in April
four boys bobbed like chunks of ice
in the chill of Moose Jaw creek.
They had flung their clothes
in crooked piles along the beach
and sprung naked and white
for the water
shrieks splashing the ridge
where three girls picnicked,
their eyes alight above the bank
to watch the bodies
twisting whitely by them
until one boy saw the trio,
bird-like heads perched in the bushes.
Five quick strokes
brought him to the shallows.
    "Hey, girls. C'mon in.
    The water's fine for bare balls."
He rose in pride to show them
but they already were in flight
    and winging for another spring.

IN THE SASKATCHEWAN

I figger somebody musta spotted it
soon as the ice went out
an give a call to the paper
cause somehow it got in the *StarPhoenix*,
just a little item in the corner,
filler I guess they call it,
but right there on the city page
where everybody'd be sure an see it.
Well, they got this gravelled lot
down on the riverbank
where people can drive in
an watch the water pour over the dam.
Course it don't get used much.
I mean how long can you sit an watch a river run by?
Except at night a course.
Then there's lotsa parking
but it sure ain't the river
they're looking at.
Anyhow by the time I drive over
I hafta leave the car
an hoof it for three blocks.
All along the bank's this real mob a people
thicker'n flies on a rotten sausage.
It takes a bit a shoving
but I make her through all right
an sure enough there it is
maybe a hundred yards from shore
sucked up against the dam
held by the undertow I spose

an alla time it's rollin over an over
but you can't see the face
not enough to do any good.
Every once in a while
a leg kinda pops up
an you can tell for sure
it don't have no shoes on.
Then a big chunk a ice
comes creaming over the dam
slams smack into it
and the whole crowd goes *ooh*.
What a buncha saps.

Anyhow it musta broke loose
for a second at least
cause it sorta flips away from the dam
an one arm comes outa the water.
I swear you'd think it was alive
an wavin right at the crowd
but the current gets it again
jammed tight against the dam
an all these yo-yos on the bank
they start babbling about who he was
an how he got there.
Well, I see nothin more is gonna happen
so I push on back through the crowd and outa there.
Ya sure won't catch me
hangin with a bunch a bloody ghouls like that.

DESIGN

The idea twisting through his mind
he took shirt and pants from the rag-bag,
tucked them in a flour sack with a ball of twine,
carried them far beyond his mother's eye.
In the gully by the tracks
he tore grass from its roots
till a pile rose large beside him
and his hands were green in blood.
He tied up sleeves and cuffs,
stuffed them full of grass,
worked the flour sack through the collar
padding to shape the whole
until a man lay there beside him.
He was on him then
pummelling his ribs
kneeing him in the groin
wrenching his tormented body
until the man lay still beneath him.
When breath had stopped rasping his throat
he grabbed the man by the ankles
heaved him up the bank to the tracks.
No one saw him drag the body
head bouncing on the ties
across the trestle,
halting above the road
that wound below and through the park.
He had his man in a choke-hold   held him
until a car came down the hill.

Waiting for the precise second
he tumbled his man from the trestle
watched him fall a coil of thrashing limbs
bounce grotesquely on the pavement
just before the veering car
cut through the guard-rail
over the bank   jammed
upside down against a tree,
its wheel spinning endlessly
in the hollow of his eye.

FIRST ELEGY

Finding the chipmunk
dead in the road
its legs squashed in gummy pavement
we scraped it into a shoebox
buried it where the scrag of pine
rose like a headstone
then climbed Sioux Bridge
leaning far out
to spit on the windshield
of every passing car

OF AN AFTERNOON

No one had seen him climbing
but he was somehow there
and it wasn't long until
the street was clogged with cars
nor long again before
a lean policeman
edged across the trestle
looking as if he'd prefer
hands and knees
to walking upright
if only there weren't
so many people
gathering to watch.
He had a grip on the upright
before he focused on the man
who hung upon the bridgework
arching high above.

"Don't do anything silly now,"
he called, feeling silly saying it.
The man never lowered his head
and he had to try again.
"Come on down, fella,
and we can talk about it."
But there were other noises now
the crowd turning below
cars skidding a block away
one voice loud above the rest,
"Jump, you crazy bugger. Jump."

It was a long minute
before the lonely echo
but only seconds
before other voices
were tasting the sound
and the sudden shock that thrilled within.
"Don't listen to em.
You can work yourself down here
an we'll walk off together."

Afterward the policeman
couldn't say how many times
he'd shouted to the shaken figure
while the crowd bound itself
into a massive plea.
He didn't know
the man had listened a full two hours
before he leapt
to meet his cheering audience.

FROM THE COLD

It's cold out shaking cold
cold like January maggots
and my neck's too big
swelling and throbbing
so when I do up the buttons
one at the collar snaps off
the cold wind coming off the river ice
goes right for my neck
frozen teeth gnawing at the throat
a shadow crosses me chill damp
and there's the sun
sitting bright sitting orange
right on top of the trestle
I go on up the hill
out on the trestle
where it's colder yet
the sun has run off
it's up on the span now
mouth open in a big orange laugh
so I go up there too
rivets round like the sun
stick out of the metal
bang at my knees
till I'm on top   it's cold
the sun has gone now
I sit down   the metal's ice on my pants
something hugging my shoulders
rubbing at them like icicles rubbing in the cold

I wait for the sun to sit down again
there's a voice coming at me
    come down   come down
something slapping my shoulders
warmth coming on them
my feet floating in the cold
boots hanging loose
so the cold is at them
running in filling them
making them swing cold and heavy
somewhere a crowd
with everybody milling
like a track meet   jump jump
like a high jump a long jump

I want my hands to clap
but the shoulders have them
cold in the palm
and the cloud goes off and the crowd
and the sun is there again
up there   not beside me
not where it should be
not laughing either
just there warm and waiting
and I jump at it so warm now
warm and turning

LOVERS AGAIN

After making love
upon the wedding bed
finding it not quite
what they had hoped
but better
than they'd feared
they chose not to sleep
but rose instead
before the sun.

Hand in hand
along the riverbank
they walked
hearing murmurs
from the water
they could only
dream of
from the flashing window
of their neon motel.

Night was shrinking
from the fragrant bank
the sky a budding rose.
While water hummed
its quiet song
once again
they came together
colouring the dawn
that burst upon the river.

MORNING RIDE

Six in the morning
and dark outside.
Wind already blowing
as I drive you to the airport.
In places snow
building again where a blade
has channeled out the road.
Open spots and ground drift
pulling the car toward the ditch.
Before the overpass
we ease around a semi
jackknifed across the road
and fishtail for Regina and the plane
that will lift you from the prairie.

In the half-light paw marks
appear from nowhere in the ditch,
move like ghosts beside us
until we see the mongrel
whiter than snow
running with us at the east
to chase the day into the sky.
It leaps a snowdrift
    rises with the vaulting sun.
The whole prairie a sudden radiance.

YARROW
(1980)

WIFE

Listen, wife, he said
using the word that Agnes hated
    I don't give a good gawdamn
    how tough things get
    We charge food and nothing else
Agnes kept her words at home
letting him work it out
    It's too easy to run up bills
    end up choked in debt
    Looket ol' McTaggart
    so far in hock he doesn't give a damn
    A piece of paper blowin down the street
    he chases it and signs his name
    Not me, wife   I still care
And Agnes caring too
would leave till later on
the matter of her name

DOUGHNUT

1

Sure they call me that
Yarrow's father told him
studying the pattern that spun
like smoke through the linoleum
    I know, Dad, but why?
    Well, he said, it's a long story
and pulled upon his pipe
    I guess uh let's just say
    I was in a nutty mood
    We were going over to Wong's
    some of us   for coffee and doughnuts
    after the pool hall closed
    only I got there first an well ...
    Well what, Dad? Tell me
but his father was intent
on blowing smoke rings
through the circle of a larger one
Just as the outer ring began to fade
the last one made it through
    Wong had just the six doughnuts
    and when the guys come in
    there weren't none left
    I'd ate them all   Wooo
    They ain't never gonna let me forget it
    Oh, said Yarrow grinning
at what his mother would say   if she knew

his father   a table pig for doughnuts
Grinning more because she'd never know

2

Yarrow had just cradled the kitten
to show the new hired hand
when Uncle Luke strode through the barn
    Just want some iron to weld the tractor hitch
    Doughnut says to try the back stall
The hired hand stood up   Doughnut?
    Yeah   Jake   Everybody calls him that
        It's a funny name   How come?
Yarrow laid the kitten by the saucer
kept his eyes upon its tongue
moist and pink beneath a froth of milk
    Well with the boy here   I don't know
        It's okay Uncle Luke Dad already told me.
    He did?   Well he always was a crazy bugger
    Anyway we was shooting pea pool
    in Magpie there   and Doughnut
    only then nobody called him that
    Doughnut he gets knocked out early
    Musta stopped off at the beer parlour
Yarrow stroked the kitten
feeling the fur soft on its neck
    Even so he gets to the Chinaman's before us
    He's the only one in the whole place

Well there's these rotating stools in there
and when we come in he swings around
real slow   had his prick out
rammed right through six doughnut holes
               Crazy bloody bugger
When the kitten squealed they looked at him
and he laughed with them   the laughter
bubbling hotly in his throat

A KITE, A SON

The kite has grown
dusty with excuses
but my son wants me
to take him kite-flying
because his father will not go
and I can find no reason
not to   or none
that he will understand

We carry the kite
into the pasture
Yarrow is certain
it will reach the sun
and I am just as sure
it will rise no higher
than I can throw it

I feel the force of gravity
release the kite anyway
and run from it
the wind somehow
thrusting it upward
Yarrow bounces beside me
his hand tugging mine
like the kite's pull
until he is gone
gliding with the kite
and slowly surely I
rise on the bright
string of his laughter

BROTHERS

Yarrow had to learn it but he loved Young Jacob
the way he'd tug a finger with chubby hands
but not the way he'd scream at sudden noises
At Easter time Yarrow held the baby chick
rubbed the down on Jacob's cheek
When the beak closed upon his ear
got the howling stopped
    Bruda Jacob said when he could talk
tumbling from his crib
and Yarrow swung him at the ceiling
taught him not to cry

In summer Yarrow took him through the fence
going farther every day
until they discovered berries
vivid in the brambles
With the first snow Young Jacob
stayed inside / eyes
as big as windows
until Yarrow showed him
how to roll the scary white
into a round and jolly man
who puffed upon a carrot

And it was Yarrow wore him out
with exploration of the pasture
brought him home the shortest way
past the hen house   the chopping block

just as Mother swung the axe
the chicken heaving back
from its severed head
whirling a crimson sphere
about their deadened feet
until the blood spilled on their boots
the circle of Young Jacob's cries
tightening like a noose

HOCKEY LESSON

Around the dugout
snow is piled
Young Jacob stands
on ankles like spaghetti
his blades pointing east and west
while Yarrow cuts another circle
on the dugout ice
stick handles like a rush
of Bentley brothers at a net

Young Jacob watches
lifts his stick and totters
slams it bangs it on the ice
    I'm Teeder Kennedy he calls
    C'mon   Pass it here
    I'm Teeder Kennedy

Yarrow sweeps toward him
lays a pass along the ice
and just as Jacob reaches
picks it up again
is gone   while Jacob
turns with awkward crooked steps
to watch him as he wheels
by and gone again

Yarrow will teach him
who he is

A MAN'S GOTTA BE TOUGH

I just don't know   Luke
since his brother came
she babies both of them
She's even got Yarrow
doin dishes after supper
She had her way   why
that'd be the only chores he'd do
Already he's the kind of kid
would step out of a shower
just to take a leak
And what's she gonna
turn him into   eh?
some kind of grocery clerk
growin up soft as snot?

ACCOMPANIED BY COYOTES

There were thirteen of them
off to the side maybe thirty yards
their tongues long in the heat
as they prowled in furnace waves
No howling   no barking
Just our footsteps on the prairie
and the padding of their feet
Jacob hadn't seen them yet
No need to worry him
I'd handle it myself

Thirteen of them   I thought   Thirteen
Still they might keep their distance
I stooped for rocks   juggling them
so Jacob wouldn't ask
I let one fall away
kept the others hard in my palms
And walked   Walked
while Jacob chuckled
at some private fantasy
the barn roof rising slowly
on the prairie sky

At the fence-line Jacob turned
Three times he clapped his hands
watched the coyotes disappear

TURNIP BUTTER

Once when I was young
Agnes Yarrow told her sons
Father took the team to town
for groceries and a blizzard came
kept him away all night
We really needed coal oil
more than groceries
We kids   you see
didn't like the dark
especially with the blizzard
shaking at our walls
but Mother had an answer
She soaked a rag in tallow
twisted it and with that light
led us through the cellar shadows
found a jar of turnips
she had canned the fall before
Then we sat around the table
in the smoky tallow glow
we peeled the turnips
cut them into halves
using kitchen knives we scraped
and ate and called it butter
butter sweet as California peaches
We forgot the night the blizzard
warm in the sweet glow of
all our turnip suns

SIGHTING

On his belly in slough grass
Yarrow watches the coyote
coming down to water
ears pricked for pasture sounds
It pauses once
steps into the water
drinks

With his rifle raised Yarrow
holds the drinking head
constant in his scope
watches dark water
ripples circling away
from the lapping tongue

He sees the splash
the frenzied tumult of water
and lowers his gun   the coyote
lifts its dripping snout
watching him across the slough
the two of them like strays
from different packs

RUNNING WITH FIRE

The slough was so dry by August
they took a crop of hay off it
Yarrow on the rack to drive the team
humming old Gene Autry songs
when well beyond his father's ear
He liked the shortcut through the pasture
the road by the old homestead
where the sod shack's standing wall
was a past of guns and outlaws
He slapped the reins
to make his getaway
gunshots and smoke in the air
but the smoke was real

He turned to flame
running at him   running
with the wind   the horses
galloped now   no need of reins
to make his getaway
Bales shook off the hayrack
as it plunged above the ruts
Yarrow fighting reins
the hayrack rising sharply
so he looked an instant on
a lake of fire the black shore beyond
then the rack went over   Yarrow
leaping   rolling
free   rolling at the flame

Up and running for the horses
Gone in a trail of broken harness
He could hear the flames
lap toward him
see his shadow change
shrink   like a burning child
And Jacob   Yarrow thought   Jacob
Jacob dead in water

He ran past the sod wall
the flames gaining
coming for him the heat
on his back hotter than sun hotter
Then the well and he was dropping
into the dark   the splash
the splash of water   cool
while above him the sky
blazed like the sun
and died again   died into clouds
into life

JULY THE FIRST

1

Yarrow counted eight of them
young guys at the door
his father laughing like a kid
enjoying their proposal
    Sure he said sure thing
    I'll try and make a comeback
    but it's gotta be in the contract
    Yarrow goes along as batboy

2

In the box of Fulton's truck
they rode together telling stories
passing round and round
a jug of homemade wine
Yarrow embarrassed once
when they offered him a shot
Before they made the turn
to the Yellowgrass Reserve
someone remembered
and pitched the bottle out
Then they hit the dirt trail
bouncing over ruts and badger holes
to the diamond in the pasture

3

Yarrow watched puppets on a hayrack
bingo in a stained canvas tent
He bet a quarter on a horse race
Indian ponies ridden bareback
galloped down a quarter-mile
Yarrow leaning through the finish line
helped his quarter multiply
Then he lay in uncut grass
with half a rhubarb pie inside
He studied miles of prairie sky
staring at a streaming cloud
that raced beyond the sun
his skin warm   alive
in blowing grass

4

His father played without a mask
jammed in tight behind the plate
one knee planted on the ground
caught well too   and hit
threw out a man at second
led his team into the money
the final game that lingered
through the creeping dusk

5

He'd never heard him scream before
his father falling from the foul
that split his thumb to bone
Yarrow rushed to hold him but
he pulled away   he strode away
blustered   laughed
    It's nothin   I can still play
    Put a chaw of tobacco on it
    some tape to hold her there
    Let's get on with the game
The colour dying slowly on his face
In the seventh inning
just before the game
was called for darkness
he hit a home run
to win it all

6

Yarrow lay in the truck box
curled against his father's chest
with singing all around
He watched the sky   the stars
a bright one in the west
pulsing like a heart

COMMUNITY SUPPER

It was your father's idea
instead of the usual fowl supper
we'd have wild duck this fall
make it fun for the whole community
Why there'd be a duck to every plate
biggest thing in the history of Magpie

So the men had the fun of
shooting the ducks

We women had the fun of
cleaning them singeing them
stripping them stuffing them
cooking and serving them

THE NEW BARN

Agnes Yarrow standing at her kitchen basin
a cracked saucer lost in her hand
looks through the sliding dusk
at the half-constructed barn
its rising beams like bones
white in the twilight

Why are barns painted red
she wonders   always red
This one could be different
and ought to be
where she must look
over dishes every day
Trimmed in white perhaps
but painted green   yes
something green against the snow
against the drought   the dust
reminding them of who they are
and why they stay

OFF BALANCE

Partway back from the barn
the gust hit him
turned him around
drove him into a drift
Doughnut got up and couldn't see
But the wind had come from home
He bent against it   the snow
like nails into his skin
the pounding wind
knocked his breath away
closed his eyes
watering   stiff
and he had come too far

The barn was bigger   the wind
might carry him back to it
or to the trough beside
He turned with the wind
the wind turning too
so he didn't know
where the barn was
nor where to keep the wind
to get him there

He had to keep moving   keep
the wind on his back
A circle would kill
a line would get him somewhere

Just walk a straight line
From his eyes he rubbed the ice
A spirit grey in the snow   a tree
like none that grew on his place
Inside he felt a prayer begin to stir
the sort of thing his wife would say

    Help me   help me   Lord
    keep me movin   movin
    snow so deep   so heavy
    one step and another
    just don't lemme fall

The crust on the snow breaking
into straw   and he
was on it in it burrowing in
the stack pale and yellow around him
like warmth as he curled   rubbing
hugging himself to warmth
to doubt

DOUGHNUT ON THE BLIZZARD

Yep   snow's so bloody thick
I couldn't hardly find
my nose between my eyeballs
Even so I could sure tell
something's in front of me
besides that wall of white
Turned out to be a straw-stack
Hell   I just dug a hole in there
and hunkered down till daylight

Well sir   maybe a week later
I'm over to the grid road
and there's Arnie Fulton
looking ready for war
What in Sam Hill's going on I wonder
He spots me and gives a holler
    Bring the .303 from the half-ton
    C'mon   Something's in the straw-stack
      Only got the one shell I say
when I get there bending down to take a look
      Holy Baldhead I say and drill a shot inside
then take off like there's a wounded bear behind
I could hardly drive away for laughin
Crazy bugger's probably still there
standin guard with a pitchfork

AND MOTHER CALLED HIM THE STALLION GROOM

I used to like the studhorse man
his stories at the supper table
his stallion black as anthracite
When he came to the farm
we always seemed to know
ahead of time   my brother and I
We climbed into the loft
watched the trail of dust
his trailer raised along the road
waited for it to turn into the yard
the stallion hot in the sunlight
nostrils flaring after father's mares

Mother would appear on the porch
drying her hands on her apron
searching until she saw us in the loft
She always insisted we stay away
while father and the studhorse man
led that great black beast
to where the mare in heat was tied

We ran from the beating sun
to play in the cool shadows
of the cistern shed
Once with my brother's help
I made it to the cistern top
wavering on the metal rim
I found a crack to look through
watched the stallion nipping at the mare

She was tethered tight against the barn
front legs hobbled on a rise of ground
the stallion pounding at her   squealing
tearing her neck with great yellow teeth
hooves beating froth and blood upon her flanks
While Father held the hackamore
the studhorse man stepped toward it
toward the penis   huge and hard and dark
I saw him do it
                    he took it in his hand
                    he held it in his hand
the penis   guided it ahead and in

I never knew till then I guess
just what it was they did
After that   I left the supper table
before the studhorse man could finish
carried dishes to the kitchen sink
plunged my hands into the water
While he unwound his secrets
I kept my eyes away from him
his hand dark upon the tablecloth

THE DANCE

In the back seat of the car
they left the kid asleep
Doughnut carried in the beer
a dozen under either arm
threading through a farmyard
packed with cars and pickup trucks
The party spilled already
out the open windows   song
and laughter like a welcome
Doughnut let his brothers
bring their music in
They could play some more
He had seen the girl
who'd watched him through the dance
eyes as bright   as moist
red lips that opened now
for him

It didn't mean a thing
he told himself
pushing in his shirt
not a gawdamn thing
even though his head
had emptied for an instant
He started down the stairs
turned to look again
breasts naked in the doorway
mouth half-open still
the wet and smiling mouth

His stomach tightened
at the sight the thought
of what she'd done
He had to walk away
He turned around
stumbled on a boy
he hardly noticed
was his son

THE HOME PLACE

Agnes looks through the window
at snow against the glass
It takes her five minutes
to force the door open
and then there is nothing
but miles of snow
smothering shed and fence
white landscape
merging somewhere
with white of sky
silence filling air
until at last she steps outside
The crust snaps
with the sound
of breaking bones

LEARNING ON THE JOB
(1986)

THIS POEM SAYS WHAT IT MEANS
(For Flash)

We have been friends
since high school days
cracking leather on defence
With you backing up the line
I played wider on the end
knowing any runner
cutting in was cut in two
Walking home after practice
we'd smoke an Old Port cigar
a little warmth passed back and forth
on the cold trek across the tracks

At university we lived together
trading puns to keep us sane
We studied in the same cramped room
one beer cooling in the window
for our midnight game of crib
Short of money every year
we talked and dreamed
about the jobs we'd have
the girls we'd marry

But dreams   we know
are mainly dreams
and different cites now
hold us apart

Most years we meet again
during holidays
in rooms that hum with relatives
Christmas drinks passed around
smiles and doing fine
everything as casual
as the smoke of cigarettes

when what I want to do
is take your hand in mine
and hold it   hold it
as I hold inside
the ways we used to be
in days we cannot have again

LEARNING ON THE JOB

The bell tinkles   the front door opens
a lady moving down the aisle
a whisper of shawls and skirts that stops
by the lipstick counter   bright fingernails
tap at the names   Crimson Delight   Vermilion Lady
Rosebud Kiss   Pastel Romance   Scarlet Fever
her nails strike the glass like castanets
I wish the boss would hurry back from coffee

She turns to look at me
her skirt a dancer's swirl
    I'll have to wait on her
I step toward her   the counter
between us all the way
She asks for Red Heat   Virgin Blush
her voice sweet   dark as maple syrup

I lay lipsticks on the counter top
tube after tube she snaps open
holds beside her mouth   her eyes
intent upon the mirror
lips red   her tongue
moist red flesh that leaps
within her mouth   touches   moistens
her upper lip   I would see more
she says   and steps behind the counter   her breasts
touch my shoulder   I
step back   Her hands remove

another tube   another
lay them on the counter-top
roll them   a dozen tubes rolling
beneath her fingertips   She selects another
removes the cap   one long red nail
strokes the base

This one   she says   this one
the lipstick strikes a line
like blood across her lip
Nodding like a fool I take her money
return the lipsticks to the showcase
Ruby Red   Saturation Pink   Midnight Fantasy
eight   nine tubes of lipstick
I watch her though the door   a dance of molten hips

THE TROUBLE WITH MARRIAGE
IS GETTING TO SLEEP

Under the covers
our bodies touch
A whisper's spark
and all at once
we fill with sighs
the empty dark

A tug a pull
a pyjama string
bound in a knot
the ties that cling
Fingers work
and fingers shift
making from night
a naked gift

A pat on the belly
a hand on the thigh
Smooth as jelly
you and I
slide together
kiss and squeeze
sheets are twisted
around our knees

A kick a tumble
a pillow's fall

a longer kiss
for the longer haul
A nibble here
a tighter squeeze
Stomach's rumble
provokes a teasing
pause
giggle   laugh

Start again

All night to do
just as we please
setting the day
the night at ease

POEM FOR A TWENTIETH ANNIVERSARY

At a conference far from home
we set out   recalling how to howl
till I brake to a stop
outside the Sutherland Hotel
Motorcycles line the sidewalk
twenty bikes that gleam like chains

I stride into the bar   hoping
the phone is near the door
Silence swings through the room
Black leather   beards
eyes like metal studs turn on me
teacher's shirt and tie   pressed slacks
only man in the room with no tattoo

    Say ... I was wondering ... uh—
    do you have a phone I could use?
He turns from pulling draught
his hand a froth of suds
    Pay phone in the lobby he says
Voices rev   a rumble of broken mufflers
I step into a different sound
where a biker chokes the phone
short nasal explosions
snap along the wires

On the floor his lady rides
his shoulder-pack   eyes closed

smoking something she has rolled
A fur halter tightens
as she drags the smoke inside
On her left breast   the tattoo of a nude
whose pelvis swells obscenely

The phone crashes down
Her eyes open   meet mine   She says
    Go ahead Mister   Enjoy yourself
    I'll really make her dance
The biker grunts a warning
                                    The shock
is me   dialing the phone   here
now   I swallow hard   and
say it   *I love you*   words
that occupy the lobby   surge
around the bikers crouched and silent
staring at my slacks
the creases razor-sharp

WHEN LIFE CAME DOWN

When life came down
to three kids fighting in the back seat
whining about who got the windows
the radio already cranked up
him driving around the block
                              again
and then again
with no parking place on Main Street
no sign of his wife
in the beauty parlour window
though she promised to be done
at least half an hour ago

he decided one more time
circled the block and saw again
no sign of her   the quarrel of kids
in the mirror   He hit the brakes
beside the beauty parlour's empty door
    Out   he said   Now   Not next week
    Right now   One ... two ...

He left them standing there
silent for a change
while he laid two lines of rubber
all the way to Number One

LOVE SHE SAID

The kids at least
weren't howling   grabbing at her
He'd been smart enough
to send them to the neighbours
You could say that much for him
Besides she wouldn't think of kids

She only had enough
to fill one suitcase
passed him in the open door
noticed his eyes   stained
like last night's coffee rings

He reached for her
as she went by
knocking his hand away
with one look
    Wait   You can't just
    leave   I mean
    don't you love me any more?

    Love   she said
    is the only disease
    that cures itself
She knew then
she was gone for good

SUNSET AND EVENING STAR

The sun is going down
and I am turning 40
when the pass comes
a shadow through the sun
burning my fingers
but I have it   the leather
throbbing in my hands

How did it happen? the doctor asks
looking at the middle finger
the way it hangs from the joint
When I tell him of the football game
his eyes move to my greying beard
but at least he does not smile
It's the tendon   he says
We call it mallet finger
If you were a concert pianist
your career would be over

Already I'm thinking of this winter
Wednesday night basketball games
my jump shot almost right
30 years after I started
falling short now   its arc gone
dropping like a wounded goose
ending evenings in the gym

and the grin is coming   spreading
till I am the doctor's chuckle

rolling with him now
40 and glad
to be worried still
about the proper arc
on a jump shot

AT THE FRONT

Mr. Miller grips his chalk
in fingers bitten at the nails
writes upon the blackboard
From the last seat   the big boy
reaches for a chalk brush
The students turn to watch him
as he stalks Mr. Miller
who is listing similes
from "In Memoriam"

The boy stoops behind him
blows a line of yellow dust
down the centre of his back
Mr. Miller's chalk has paused
in the middle of a word
If he turns around now   if
he turns
around
if
Mr. Miller squeezes chalk
in fingers bloodied at the nails

CROSSING AMERICA

I

On board the Union Pacific
pulled toward the west
I watched the line of smoke
from the window of my berth
pretended Navajos
sent signals through the dark

Or when my parents were asleep
put on my clothes again
and sat in the observation car
studied businessmen who smoked
and waved their glasses   stretching
stories from the past

Once I even stole out to the platform
saw the solitary lights of farms
shouted at the whistle-stops
waving like a presidential candidate
promising tomorrow   while America
retreated into night

II

On the edge of Arizona
the train bumped and shook
jerking to a halt

Pressed against the window I saw
a half-ton battered to its side
a load of cabbages like severed
heads rolled into the ditch
Already at the cab
a crowd was gathering
I stared at the seat across the aisle
till I heard a trainman's footsteps
     Was anybody killed?
   No he said just an Indian
All around me the people
relaxed chattering again
as others climbed aboard

III

Train cars clanking to a start
links of chain that hold us
as we move into the future
hurled toward the sunset
California
and the dark

CARTOGRAPHER
(For Lorna)

I walk stubble
crackling underfoot
the sounds sharp against the wind
whirling over 500 miles
of uncharted prairie   moaning
across the cracked steer skull
wedged into a badger hole

The wind leans into me
rises another wailing octave
until I feel one horizon
shift toward the other

Here beneath the bone-white sky
the air is full of poems
but I walk on alone
hurry to the river bank
its scant calligraphy of willows
My prairie now is yours
your poems have made it so

CAPTAIN HAINES RETIRED

Rake in hand   the old man
lifts his collar to the breeze
His feet set upon the grass
as if he strode a pitching deck
he leans toward his tilted picket fence
lifts the rake   throws it
to the limit of his reach
then draws it slowly in
hand over hand   a fisherman
sure of what his nets will yield

His catch piles up around his feet
as he lifts and leans
extends the rake and pulls it in

The wind begins to swirl
leaves leap about his feet
break the surface of the lawn
green waves rushing from the wind

He glances at the sky
where branches creak like a ship's rigging
then from a baggy sweater pocket
draws his pipe
Hands cupped against the wind
he fills his mouth
with a taste more pungent than
the smell of burning leaves

He leans upon his rake
The wind will fall   the leaves
will settle on the grass
The old man   smoking   waits
to rake the dead leaves in

KLONDIKE FEVER
(1992)

SLEDDING ON PARK AVENUE

We buy all the dogs we can find
four Saint Bernards and two Newfoundlands.
When the harness is finished
we begin to train them
night after night in Manhattan
dragging an old bobsled
loaded with lumber for weight,
our runners sparking through slush.

One night we grate onto Park Avenue,
a policeman's horse rearing above us,
hooves striking the sky,
and he's yelling like a foreman:
"What are you doing?   Just what the hell
do you think you're doing?"

"Training for the Klondike, of course."
He holds his horse steady on the sidewalk.
"The gold craze," he says.
"You and half the population
gone berserkers.
You'll freeze to death up there.
I'd like to hold you in jail for a year,
but that's up to the Humane Society."

The reins tight in his hands,
he laughs at our protests.
"It's cruelty to animals.

Harness is for horses,
not dogs."

The judge disagrees.
He sets us free at once,
investing five hundred dollars
for a share of our gold.

LEAVING ROWENA

The engine shakes on the rails,
steam hisses along the platform,
people swarm for the Pullmans.
Men push past, bump us,
jam for seats.

I bend to kiss her, her arms on my back
pull me tight, her body hard against mine,
the sweet taste of her mouth. I hold
her a moment, my cheek on hers.
No, must leave, I pull away,
the crowd surges between us.
I stride toward the train, glance
once over my shoulder, her hand
waves from an island in the flow.

Onto the train, squeeze
by two men at the door,
hurry down the aisle, drop
into an empty seat
in the middle of the coach.
The train jerks, sways.

And then, my cheek tingling, I touch it,
her tears damp on my skin.
Press against the window.
She's still there, waving.
A ray of sunlight strikes her hair,
gleams like a vein of gold, the train
wrenches me away.

EVERYWHERE ON THE GLACIER

Everywhere on the glacier
snow burns in the sun.
We wear smoked glasses
and go blind with staring,
cover our faces with handkerchiefs
—small holes cut to see through—
but nothing helps.

The only relief
is rubbing our eyes
and they swell like boils.
After a few days, mine feel like
I've scoured them with sand.

It's Weiden decides
to improvise a salve
from bacon fat.
The salt
nearly finishes him.
He tears at his eyes, wanting
to leave them behind in the snow.

Still he carries on, like the rest of us,
keeping busy with the sleds, anything
to occupy the hands, the mind.
Weeks later I see myself
staring from a mirror, my lashes
rubbed completely away.

ACCIDENTS

I

Weiden late for supper,
Boyer says, "He's pouting again.
Let's just go ahead and eat.
Hell, we'll enjoy it more without him."

Two hours later
we send out a search party.
We find his tracks—circling
then tacking across the snow
like he's searching for something.
The last thirty yards
lead straight to a crevice.

"Terrible," says Boyer, "a terrible accident."
His eyes leap like fire when no one speaks.
"But just an accident," he says.
"That's all. The last one we'll have."

No one knows what to do.
Murtha comes up with a prayer,
a few odds and ends
he remembers from Sunday School.

Then a minute's silence
and we stumble back to camp.

II

Two weeks more and still
no sign of the glacier's end.
"God," says Boyer, "I'd like the feel
of earth beneath my feet again.
I've had it up to here with ice."

Another day and Boyer
drops into a crevice so narrow
a one-legged man could hop across.
He falls no more than ten feet
but his neck is broken.

Right behind him, Murtha
swears he never made a sound.

RUNNERS

"We're finished," Eagen tells us.
He slides a hand over the sled runner,
the ragged steel tearing at his mitt.
"They're worn out. Done.
Pulling these sleds is like
dragging tombstones over gravel.
We might just as well shoot the dogs."

"No," says Murtha. "We'll go on
and we'll make it
cause there's nothing else to do.
So you can quit your gawdamned whining."
He spits, almost nails Eagen in the foot.

Eagen stares at the gob
a bare inch from his boot,
already frozen solid.

My God, Eagen will kill him.
He steps forward, hands
reaching for Murtha. He has him
in an embrace.
"That's it. You've got it."

Murtha and I give him a hand,
hoist one of the sleds on end,
and he pours water down the runner
where it freezes, the surface
slick as glass.

NOT TO MENTION BLACK FLIES AND OTHER BUGS

Everything we eat is flavoured with mosquitoes.
We bake our flapjacks under tin plates
and lift the plates to turn them,
finding dozens of mosquitoes, everyone
of them wanting his share of the syrup.

Making bread, we hold the dough
in a cloth bag, knead it with one hand,
the other holding the bag shut.
Always the finished dough is dark,
mottled with bodies like raisins.

Our tents have flaps and netting
which only keep the mosquitoes
swarming at our heads.
We try to smoke them out,
suffocate in our sleeping bags.

At daybreak we get up and find
one of our malamutes missing.
"Carried off by mosquitoes," says Murtha.
"Just wait. We'll find him along the trail
—all the blood sucked away."

HORMAN, DAVIS, MORRIS

I

They took three week's provisions,
but they've been gone longer than that.
It's time we went looking.
"I don't know," says Pittman.
"They're supposed to be exploring, sure,
but they're probably lolling around the countryside,
taking it easy somewheres
while we slave in the shaft.
We strike gold, I guarantee it,
they'll be back the same day."

The next morning
four of us begin the search.
Kodiak picking out a trail,
we fight our way for twenty-five miles,
the country tough as a rock pile.

Sniffing the air, Kodiak whines,
runs ahead. Beside a stunted spruce
we find the tent. No sign
of Horman, Davis, Morris.

II

We await their return, lie
that night in their tent,
uneasy thoughts shaking our sleep.
In the morning we yell, shoot
our rifles into the vast silence, wait
while echoes circle and fade.
We build a fire and smother it
till smoke lifts a signal
high in the clear air.

Nothing answers.

We debate our next move,
end by following Kodiak
who leads us to a gash
torn from the mountain's side,
the fresh wound of an avalanche
and never again
will there be any sign
of Horman, Davis, Morris.

MURTHA ON THE VALUE OF GOLD

"It's nothing but a lousy yellow metal.
Worth not a bloody cent more
than any other stone in this gawdamned creek.
You can't burn it, can't eat it,
and sure as snow it won't get us home.
From this day on, I waste
not one bloody minute looking for the stuff.
Give me the richest mine in the Klondike
and maybe—just maybe—I'll pause long enough
to take a crap in it. Yeah, then
wipe my ass with the deed. That's all.
Only thing in this Godforsaken land
that interests me is getting out."

WAITING

There's only one hope,
Murtha and I decide.
Soon as enough snow falls
we make a try for the Pacific.

Still there's Merrill,
burning, tossing in fever.
We cannot move him, will not
leave without him.

Our days are spent catching fish,
smoking them in strips above the fire.
At night we lie in our bedrolls,
listen to Merrill's threadbare breathing.
Outside, snow buries our sleds.
If we stay here all of us will die.

When he shakes the fever's grip,
Merrill looks at us once
as if he understands.
The next day he
dies without a murmur.

WHAT WE HAVE TO DO

The fire is right, coals glowing.
I wait, in my hand the axe,
its head flat as a hammer.

Murtha, always thinking,
harnesses the dog.
He grips the straps. Pittman holds
its attention with a sliver
of bone, the only food in camp.

I step behind the husky,
raise the axe like a sledge,
put all my weight behind it,
drive the hammer down on the head
—bones crack, I hear them crack.
Eyes bulging, the dog
drops without a whimper.

Pittman bends beside it, flicks
a knife across its throat, the blood
steaming on the snow.
Barking then, the other dogs
fight to reach the carcass.
Murtha, Wilson kick them off,
Pittman already cutting meat.

ALMOST DONE

At least six weeks
when three should've
brought us to the Copper River.
I know I'll die
on this Godforsaken glacier,
huddled in a bank of snow.

Yet something keeps me moving,
plodding forward, straining on,
the darkness all around.
So easy just to lie down and rest.
But got to help the dogs, help them
drag our burden, hardly notice
when we hit a long incline,
it means something I've forgotten,
we kill another dog for food, push on,
always down through the endless dusk,
almost done now, don't expect
to make it home again, know
it's nearly over,
we're finished now, done,
I'll never see Rowena—and then
a glare on the horizon, I curse
the light that stings my eyes.

Ice brushed clean,
polished by wind, the white
sheen in the dim twilight

shines brighter than day
as we toil our way toward
the horizon where a thin streak
rides below the dusky sky, widening,
widening as we drag on down
toward it, the long blue line
shifting to water,
to sea.

SNOWED IN

I

Snow like eiderdown, but cool,
damp on our faces, my breath
lifting the flakes, wafting
them upward a moment where
they mingle with a million more,
the night turning white with them,
white and turning, drifting down,
everything a shifting haze,
a sea of white slipping over me,
spreading, enfolding me while
I slide into something
that resembles sleep.

II

Everything soft and hazy, shades
of white clean and pure as bandages,
my mind too tired for thought.
Till something moves. I wonder
where I am, but something's moving,
something white passing near.
I seem to be alone,
to lie on something white.
Sheets, white sheets stretched
tight, and then a woman

moving, a woman in a room,
a nurse, my God, a nurse, I can't
make sense of this,
give in again to sleep.

THE NURSE

Goodness no, you've been here a week,
sleeping nearly all the time
and talking like a wild man.
Rowing, you were, rowing a boat, I guess—
What? Oh, I see. Your wife. Her name's Rowena.
Yes, well, today is April 18th,
you understand—of course, 1899.
This is Sitka Hospital, Sitka, Alaska.

Oh, my goodness gracious, certainly not me.
It was Captain Adams found you.
He runs the *Wolcott*, the U.S. cutter,
it patrols along the coast—
Smoke. That's right. It was
your fire that brought them in—
Oh, they did everything they could.
What matters is they got you here at once—

No. No, I'm sorry ... but Mr. Murtha,
Mr. Pittman, and Mr. Wilson are alive.
The other three were dead in their sleeping bags.
It must have been a peaceful way to die.
Drifting off to sleep, they'd never know a thing.

Oh, I didn't mean that.
I'm sure you'd want to know—
Of course, we'd tell you
if there was anything to fear.

Now, please, lie back down.
Mr. Dietz, I assure you
everything will be quite all right.
Why, next week, there's a steamer to Seattle.
I expect you'll be on it.

RUNNING IN DARKNESS
(2006)

YOUNG BOY, FLEEING

I remember running out pyjama-clad to the back step.
Mrs. Loverin, our neighbour across the alley fence,
wheeled from hanging her Monday wash.
I'd been sick with fever, asleep in my parents' room,
the black oak desk beside the bed, crooked
light from the cracked window, the dark cubby-hole

where the letter opener gleamed a warning.
My chosen dinner finished, brown sugar, sweet
and golden, all of it spooned away, a thin layer
of Sonny Boy cereal congealed in the curve of the bowl,
I woke to the rumble of waves, blankets rumpled,
rolling toward me, raging wool waves

foaming over my face, pulling me under.
I flailed and twisted, fought free, ran past my aproned mother,
her hands in the sink, slicing the skin from potatoes.
Wrenching the door wide—shock
of cold boards on bare feet—I screamed
and screamed, They're going to kill me help me please.

Mrs. Loverin, a wooden clothespin caught in her teeth,
her puckered face like that of her budgie, a seed in its beak,
one sock dangling, her basket of clothes dropped in the dirt
as she turned to me with a look I'd never seen,
and behind me my mother, my loving innocent mother,
faltered at the door, the knife ablaze in her hand.

UNCLE ANDREW

"When he was your age," my aunt said,
"your uncle never once brushed his teeth."
Every night and in the evenings playing crib
he kept both plates in a shaving mug by the bed.

I used to grin when he relaxed, his mouth closing,
elastic lips collapsing back upon themselves,
the jut of his chin all but touching his nose,
but my aunt turned from the cards and shook her head.

He looked after me once while she was out at bingo.
I chuckled at the way his lips opened and folded
around the bottle he pulled from a brown paper bag.
"You think something's funny here?" he asked.

He set his bottle down and leaned toward me,
the slap like a two-by-four against my cheek.
I started to cry and ran for the bedroom.
"Stay there," he said, "or I'll cut off your cock."

It was hours before I fell asleep on the damp pillow.
When I awoke my uncle had already gone to work,
the aroma of cinnamon buns calling me to the kitchen.
I stayed at the bathroom mirror, brushing and brushing my
    teeth.

FALLING

April 8th, 1954

for Larry

When we rode our bikes
to school that day,
we didn't know
there'd soon be people
stopped on busy crosswalks
staring at the sky, the Harvard trainer
colliding with the North Star which twisted
down, the pilot's knuckled hands
holding it above the elementary
school, thirty-five people drawing
sudden breaths, the bigger plane
bursting open, a silver wing
sliding off, the explosion
plunging passengers into the exhibition
grounds, the golf course, the back
yard of a woman hanging
out her wash, flames like water
pouring down, the fuselage
shattering a house, another woman
working there, a cleaning woman
is what the papers said, but no, they got it
wrong, she wasn't that, she was
the mother of my friend
and she was dead that morning,
the very day we rode
our bikes to school,

pumping hard, lifting
off the curbs, a breathless
instant in the air

JUBILEE

The year we went to California was 1955,
my summer beneath a coat of Clearasil.
Before we started that July, my father
acquired three hundred paper matchbooks,
each bearing three sheaves of wheat,
a gilded windblown banner proclaiming
"Saskatchewan's Golden Jubilee."
He planned to celebrate along the way,
to let the Americans know about our home.
"Pop," I said, cringing in the back seat,
"nobody's gonna want your stupid penny matches."
What I meant, of course, was Don't embarrass me.

From the Montana border to the San Francisco Bay
he gave them out every time we stopped,
to gas jockeys, waitresses, motel clerks,
to every chance passerby in every whistle-stop.
They responded with handshakes, extra fries,
soft drink refills, with etched souvenir glasses
in Salt Lake City; coloured prints of western scenes
in Winnemucca; with rolls of nickels for
the Reno slot machines. Through the windshield
I watched the transformations, faces
masked for work, open and alive again.
Everywhere we stopped, they stopped,
suspended from the day, smiling, wondering
if we knew their cousins in Vancouver,
if we'd had much snow this summer,
if he'd stay that Saska-word again.

In Redding, California, I saw a girl my age,
a pert brunette, peroxide streaked hair.
She looked as cool as the peak of Mount Shasta,
and just as distant, far too cute for me,
but I slid from the backseat. "Pop," I said,
"those matches, could I maybe have a few?"

P.S. Her name was Merrilee. For three incredible
years her letters bound California to Saskatchewan.
Thanks, Pop. Thanks a million.

HICK

The college girls
seemed imports
from a foreign world

His English prof
charting novels at the board
never wore a bra
and he knew he blushed
when she mentioned phallic symbols
Once she caught him   circled
hovered   as she spoke
    Take Hemingway's *The Sun Also Rises*
    The name   Robert Cohn   Surely you can see it
    Might we have some symbolism here?

While other students
turned to look
   the girls   the smiling girls
he felt that he
was everybody's fool
    Cajones   Surely
    you see it now   Cajones
    You might just explain
    the significance of that

    Certainly   You're the one
    I'm talking to

The blood rushing to his face
he groped for any kind of mask
    Back home   he said   there's cows and bulls
    but I'd have to say
    your Mr. Cohn was a steer
His mouth   dry as straw

THE SUMMER I WORKED CONSTRUCTION

Two hundred and seventy-six miles from Moose Jaw
to Maidstone, but I was driving my father's car the wrong way,
weekend over, shovel and gravel waiting for Monday,
and you were there with your mom in the little house,
the cellar packed with darkness, trap door by the couch,
where I lay, thrilled by your quiet breathing
—waves on a moonlit lake sliding to shore—
but here was no moon, and you
were on the other side of the wall, though hand
in hand we'd walked out of town that evening,
puffs of dust rising together at every step,
hushed prairie and bush, one magpie in the dusk
just a whisper of black, gliding low
at the edge of vision, your shoulder
pressed against mine, we talked of when
we'd meet again, how we'd manage
our lives, wanting the magic to last, your hand
still in mine, though both of us knew it was over,
and here I was, back on the pavement, driving
through Paynton, the town I knew as a boy,
the grain elevator where my uncle worked in the '40s
burnished now by the sinking sun, no one knowing
that one day it would fall, collapsing,
a fury of splinters and dust, an expert
imported from somewhere else
to manage the blast.

THAT DAY

My afternoon class already canceled,
I sat in our basement suite at noon,
making a sandwich, considering
which book to begin from those on my list,
but the radio was on—interruptions—and soon
I was spreading peanut butter on toast,
the knife moving senselessly back and forth
like a weather vane caught in a wind
that changes and changes again.

I left my lunch by the kitchen sink, walked out
to the '56 Chev, its tank nearly empty, drove
all the way across town to the gas station
whose owner once supplied my roommate and me
with buckets of used oil for our old junker
that burned black gold like a wildfire at the well.
Filled the tank there, a debt of loyalty,
though at first I thought the owner was gone,
his face like a stranger's, his hand on the pump
like an automaton—he didn't seem to remember or care.

All afternoon I drove through the city,
turning at corners I'd never seen,
streets I'd never known, rows of houses,
bungalows with white siding, exactly
the kind I might some day own, but now
they could all be awaiting the wrecker's ball,
their groomed lawns stretching flat and lifeless,

like him, surrounded by rushing men, doctors
and agents, frantic for hope, his body
laid out on that gurney in Dallas.

STARTING OUT TOGETHER
for Gwen

We brake and stop for a solitary moose,
its hulking shoulders, its dark bulk just visible
in a thrill of moonlight by the lake.
Then we hear our song on the car radio.

We're deep in the park, miles from the Narrows.
our honeymoon cabin where light dies at midnight,
the generator stilled, cold stars shaking above.
Car doors flung wide, we step out together,

dance on the band of broken pavement,
aspens quaking in the car's dim light,
beyond them, black woods, rock and decay,
the eyes of animals, awake and waiting.

Warm in each other's arms, aching with love,
through August air chilled by bitter wind
we sway together easy as a promise,
footsteps in concert, the thrum of music,

the reassuring hum of the idling engine,
shadows and moonlight, silent pines around us,
while somewhere, north of the park, an animal,
alone and in pain, tears at its paw in the dark.

CLOSING TIME

After supper I drive with my son to the lake,
enter the dark cabin, the heat of summer
gone, winter crouched beneath the beds.
Floorboards shift like thin ice underfoot
as we pack the food, cover windows
with plywood sheets.
               We walk together
to the water, a frigid moon floating there, my son
pitches a rock that makes the moonlight vanish.
He shouts in celebration, up beyond his bedtime,
but it will freeze tonight, the pipes need draining.

I turn the pressure system off, pull the hose
from cold water—it comes out stiff and brittle,
like a frozen snake. I lay it on the bank, remove
the foot-valve, watch the water gush, its sibilant rush
the only sound in the chill night—my son

is gone. I wheel around, nothing moving,
stumble down to the lake, not a wave, moon
and stars like frost motes on black water, I scrabble
up the rocks, running in darkness, call his name,
willing my voice calm, mustn't frighten him   or me,
up the porch steps, snap on cabin lights,
every room empty, I dash outside,
the stars still ice on the lake, the moon
is gone, a cloud, I know, a cloud
is all, I swing around, caraganas

derelict and motionless,
I suck in my breath to howl
his name,
                    the backhouse door
slaps shut, and here he comes

pausing where I clutch
the porch rail, chest
heaving.
                    You look away
for just an instant:
this is how it happens.

WITH HIS TROUSER BOTTOMS ROLLED

When I pull into the driveway, the kids come running,
shouting before I'm out of the car: "Grandpa had an accident!"
I picture my withered father at the wheel of his Plymouth
regarding the road from under the steering wheel's arc,
the car creeping through a light, slammed sideways, crushed.

"Is he okay?" "Sure, he's gonna be fine," says my daughter.
"Mom took him to the hospital. We had to wait in
    emergency."
"Not for long," my son adds, breathless, "just for the x-ray.
The doctor said at his age he shouldn't be riding a bike."

What's this? My father whom I've never seen on a bicycle,
the man who took me into the park with my first two-wheeler,
told me, "Get on, you learn best by doing," and gave me a
    shove.

The kids say he tossed them his cane, straddled my bike, asked
for a push, wobbled across our lawn, almost across the
    neighbour's.

When the broken rib mends, they add, he's going to try it
    again.

HISTORY
for Larry Hadwen

The names have rung in his mind
since he was chosen to go,
Birkenau, Treblinka, Dachau, Auschwitz.
He is one of fifteen teachers
who walk through the gates of death,
who will walk out again.
He knows he will see the mass graves
where no names mark the place of the Jews,
the gas chambers, the ovens, the chimneys
from which their ashes fell.

Surrounded by electrified wire,
he gazes at tree-lined streets, tidy barracks.
Inside a building he walks slowly by a case of shoes,
oxfords, boots, loafers, piles of them,
most worn, the leather cracked, a few
looking as comfortable as those he now wears.
Brogans, sandals. A pair of baby booties.
He turns away. Stops.
Wonders what he's staring at.
A dark mass, black, gray, every shade of brown ...
Hair, mounds of human hair. And there at the top,
the blonde braid of a child,
the ribbon still around it. And he
is weeping, the tears
like ash on his cheeks.

WATCHING HER

When first my daughter took the stage
for Doris Sitter's School of Dance,
the year's finale, "Every Child A Star,"
she wobbled on her toes, and waved,
her mom and I seated in the first row.
She kept dancing, learned to tap and kick,
to spin in unison with other whirling figures,
sure moves in floodlit grace, her mom and I
watching from shadows underneath the balcony.

In high school she quit the dancing
and made the mixed curling team,
told us there was one rule,
on Tuesday nights and Thursdays
we were not to enter the Hillcrest rink.

Just once I trespassed in the lounge,
bought a beer and edged toward
windows overlooking sheets of ice.
I found the red and gold team, spied
my daughter sliding from the hack, stretching
to release—but her friend, the skip, looked up,
I ducked away, pausing a second at the bar,

my eyes shut, I see her slide, fluent and sure,
her rock skimming the ice, she rises, follows it,
watches as it strikes the shot rock, peels off
and hits another, clears the house, settles

three inches from the button. My daughter
raises her hands above her head, taps
her feet, triumphant, pirouettes and smiles,
then, yes, she's waving up at me.

WHY I WAS SEATED IN THE MIDDLE OF THE FRONT ROW AT THE SASKATCHEWAN CENTRE OF THE ARTS

Aunt Aggie had spent the whole morning shopping for dresses.
Tired, sick of high heels, hungrier than a hog, she
ordered spaghetti and meatballs for lunch at Alfredo's.
The waiter was Scottish and slow bringing the meal.
She hurried to get it inside her. Good food,
she always says, won't do no one no good
if it just lies like a worm on the plate.
She had arranged to meet Myrtle Belle in the mall
directly beneath the statue of the third Ukrainian lady
and she was rushing her meal when one string of spaghetti
did a jig on her fork, sprayed tomato sauce on her pink blouse.
She patted the fabric with a damp serviette,
cleaned off her plate and scurried for Eaton's,
hoping to find spot remover in Main Floor Notions.
While handing over $9.99 for a bottle
no bigger than a munchkin's thimble,
she saw the sales clerk's mouth flop open
as if she were ready to swallow a rabbit.
Aunt Aggie swung around and there,
directly across the aisle in Men's Wear,
no more than five feet away, stood
Tony Bennett, thumbing a pack of silk handkerchiefs.
"Good gravy glory me," Aunt Aggie yelped, and Tony Bennett
compelled by the squeal in her voice, turned and found
himself staring at a seventy-six year old woman
whose blouse was bedaubed with tomato sauce.
Aunt Aggie was close enough, she could have tousled his wig.

She blushed, glanced at his packet of hankies, blurted,
"Nose rags to riches!" and ran for the mall.
It took more than a minute to catch her breath
before she told Myrtle Belle what a fool she'd been.
Tonight her living room sofa was as close
as she'd get to any concert. Holy old Hanna,
she couldn't let Tony Bennett spot her in the crowd.
There was no telling what the man might do.

HE LOVED TO HEAR HER PLAY

Sometimes at night my mother appears in the old house,
lingering a while by the long wall in the living room

where the upright Heintzman piano stood
the year my aunt was gone and loaned it to her.

A pale glimmer of light from the corner streetlamp
illuminates a grey pillow on the chesterfield,

but black and white ivory keys remain invisible
as they would be if they were here in darkness,

the piano long ago reclaimed and gone
—who knows where so many years after?—

my mother drawing a straight back chair toward the wall,
settling on it, her back arched, hands extended, rising,

she begins to play, agile fingers gentle on the keys,
the music, slow and elegant, an old-time waltz, perhaps,

familiar faces, relatives I haven't seen in ages,
some I only recognize from photographs,

grandparents, so many aunts and uncles, all of them
in pairs tonight, swaying to the rhythm

of the tune my mother plays my father,
a melody he may not hear again for years.

EVENING AT EXTENDICARE

Seven o'clock. The dining hall swept clean,
tables pushed away, I maneuver my father
into a hushed semi-circle of wheelchairs.
Other residents sit stiffly on benches and
dinner chairs in rows before the open floor,
before the band, Andy's Midnight Combo.

In fluorescent glare, "By the Light of the Silvery Moon,"
the band plays, a thin vocalist, his quavering voice
held fast by the violin that rises, falls behind him.
"Jeepers Creepers," "Yes Sir, that's My Baby,"
"Wrap Your Troubles in Dreams," and two women
walk into each other's arms, begin to sway.
Nursing aides look for others who can waltz,
lead them to the floor, launch into the old songs.
"Let Me Call You Sweetheart." One wheelchair
is rolled before the band, turning slowly with the tune.
My father's fingers drumming leather arms,
he leans toward me. "We could do that," he says.

I stand, feel people watching me,
feel a blush crawl above my collar, shrug,
wheel him forward, step awkwardly behind,
and we enter the circle of dancers,
my cheeks flaming. "Ain't We Got Fun?"
          But I can do this,
I slap my feet in rhythm,
                    swing him
                 to the left,

                              the right,
                    spin him in a circle
                 at the centre of the floor.

The music holds the old smile on his face
and all at once I think that I remember
a smiling man, a child at someone's wedding dance,
the child lifted through the lilting air, held firmly,
the man gliding over shining floors, graceful loops,
his slim legs stepping, reaching, closing,
the child laughing in his arms,
and somewhere beyond, a lush violin.
"I Can't Give You Anything But Love."

MY FATHER'S SHOES

They lie discarded in the hall closet
where they were tossed some years ago,

the pair of Rockports, a discontinued style,
leather more orange than brown, worn soles,

pushed down heels, folded and split.
I lift and hold the shoes a moment,

stroke the furrowed leather, set them down
and slip them on, shocked to feel

how well they fit. I note a darker polish
over stains which show like pentimento,

or like the fading figure of a man
who walks away, never looking back,

though he pauses once in falling snow.

WITNESS
(2009)

IN THE GALLERY

His parents have moved on to the next wing,
but the boy remains to gaze at the dark horse
running in twilight, all four hooves in the air,
the sky a dull shroud over dun fields below.
He wishes he rode the horse, could turn it aside,
but there are no reins, and it runs between rails
that shine brighter now as the long train looms.

The boy turns to the glare of the headlamp, smoke
peeled away by wind and the speed of the train,
looks again at the galloping horse—the train closer now—
and he thinks of the drive out of New Brunswick,
the sharp curve in the road, his father's headlights
sweeping the ditch, blood and the huge black hulk
of a moose crippled in the weeds, broken
glass glinting beside it, then gone in the gloom.

This is no moose, but a horse, spirit and power,
muscle hurling it forward, no hesitation
as it plunges toward the light, and he wonders
if maybe there might be a chance ...
The boy is stunned, fixed, oil on canvas.
Behind him his father appears at the door,
calls his name, pauses, calls it again,
the boy breathless before the painting.

APRIL PILGRIMAGE

Shrinking crusts of snow in the ditch
where only shadows reach.
A hitchhiker sits on a soiled backpack,
his thumb isn't working well today.

He stares into the pavement's shimmering glare,
bright figures moving Christ-like on the waves,
knees rise and fall, rise and fall as they approach.
Bicycles, he realizes, a caravan of bicycles,
floating on the highway's haze, they glide and grow,
women with bandanas, men with flowing beards
and pony tails, uh huh, superannuated hippies
on the move to somewhere, carts behind their bikes
piled high with bundles wrapped in blue tarpaulins.

The hitcher stands to watch them come, everyone
in jeans, of course. He cocks his thumb.
"I could ride on a cart," he says. "A crossbar.
Even handlebars would do." No one speaks.
In the wire carrier of the final bike
a mongrel bares its teeth and snarls.

FATHER AND SON: RITE

It often happened in the kitchen,
say an hour or so after supper,
when you were starving again, the lid
throbbing above the pot of Kraft Dinner,
me on my way to the fridge for a Coke.

I'd flourish my hand at shoulder height.
You'd give me a grin like a paperboy taking a tip,
plant your feet, seize my hand, straining, one tooth
pressing your lower lip, while I swung your arm down.

I still remember the smile, the light
that blazed in your eyes that August day
we stood by the kitchen sink, sweat
beading our biceps, hands trembling, my grip
tightening, as you slowly put me down.

That was twenty years ago and even now
with those days gone away, the miles sliding by,
I'd issue the challenge, square off in the kitchen,
no more hope of winning now than living forever.
Ah, but the feel for an instant: your hand gripping mine.

BREAKING UP

I

It's a month since his mother left.
Jamie glares across the Lipton soup,
laughs when I tell him to eat.
"You cook like a pimp," he says.

In seconds we're both yelling.
When I find myself grabbing for his neck,
I go outside instead, stand
in the back yard, gulp
the cold air, hands
wild and empty.

II

The first game in the midnight league.
The stick-handling, the stops and
cuts, the rushes up the ice,
I snap a pass to my buddy on the wing,
movement sweet as music,
slick as sex.

Four minutes into the first period
the whistle blows. I coast to a stop,
heave for breath. Next thing
I'm flat on the ice, back numb

from a cross check. I roll over,
look up at number seventeen.
He's got at least five inches on me
and probably fifty pounds.

"Well," he says, "what you gonna do about it?"
I look at him for maybe three seconds.
It's an easy decision. "Nothing."

On my next shift seventeen
sweeps toward our end, grinning
like he owns the ice—and me.
As he skates past, I back off a step,
then take him with an elbow in the throat,
snap his head back, smash
him into the boards
where something breaks.

III

I stretch out
in a hot bath, back pulsing.
On the way to bed, I stop
outside the door of Jamie's room.
He's breathing soft and easy
as a stabled colt.

Then the walk down the hall,
my own room bare of furniture
except for the king-size bed
where I'll sweat
on sheets of ice.

THE LESSON

"Keep your chin down," he said,
"your left in his face, like this,
always jabbing at his eye.
Have your right hand ready,
coiled here like a snake, eh? Ha!
When he blinks, give it to him."

I learned that lesson well.
From grade four to eight
I never lost a fight
and I fought a lot.

I fought an awful lot.
My hands were rough and sore,
my knuckles scraped and raw.
Yeah, my father taught me how.

BORIS KARLOFF REMEMBERS REGINA

One tires of playing monsters, certainly, but it's a living, and I shan't forget what it is to be without funds. Years ago I was in the employ of a touring company, working our way across the Canadian plains until we came to a city of moderate size. The capital of Sask-atch-je-wan. We had the afternoon off, a group of thespians testing our versatility in canoes, when a storm came up, great spinning clouds, green and thick as vomit, wind tearing at the lake until the water rose like a typhoon, and still we must have been on the storm's edge, because back in town everything was knocked flatter than the horizon. Which, in that part of the world, is extraordinarily linear. Indeed. And people standing around in a stupor as if the Lord had clubbed them senseless.

In this business, the show must go on. We decided to offer a benefit. The very next night drew a good-sized crowd, though 'twasn't easy being funny. They laughed in the right places, certainly, but all I could think of was what I'd seen the day before. People collapsing in the street. One woman staring at the remains of her home, her hands in her eyes as if she could rub them away with everything they'd seen. Was she in the crowd that night, another voice in all that laughter?

Comedy may get the laughs, I thought, but it's no match for horror. Something there to contemplate. Which is precisely what I was doing, mulling it over in the wings, when I missed my next cue. That was nineteen hundred and twelve, and let me make one thing clear. I've not missed a cue since. Nor a monster part either. There's much to be said for steady work.

LIAR

Daddy, it's Daddy
who puts me to bed
when Mommy has meetings at night.

He tucks the covers under my chin
and reads me *Alice in Wonderland*.
He says he'd show Alice a thing or two.

When he's done reading he turns out the light
and lies down beside me, so close
I can hear his heart beat.

His breathing gets louder and louder.
Then he rolls toward me.
Here, he says, touch me here.

When he goes away, he never
says good night. In the morning
he won't even look at me.

I told Mommy today
and she hit me and started to cry.
She said I was a little liar,

I should love my Daddy
and, Lord, I better behave
—she's got a meeting tonight.

RISKING THE DREAM
(an excerpt)

1945

The older man leans across his desk, scowling.
"Nigger," he says, "what you think you doing here?
Get along now, boy. This cafe for white folks only."
Then he is an abusive fan, a hostile teammate,
a snotty hotel clerk, a railroad conductor
slinging insults, scorn, while the black man sits,
unmoving, rigid, his huge hands clenched.
Judas Priest, thinks Rickey, he wants to hit me.
Can he possibly be the man for the job?

Major league baseball is a white man's game.
No black's been allowed to play since 1891,
but Branch Rickey can't forget Charles Thomas,
the only Negro on his college team, their fight
for a hotel room, the player finally
allowed to have a cot in Rickey's room,
but unable to sleep, rubbing one hand against the other
muttering, "If I could only make 'em white."
As if he could scour the black skin from his flesh.

Now Rickey has a plan for his Brooklyn Dodgers.
In his office is a rookie from the Negro League,
a letterman from U.C.L.A., a college man,
yes, that's got to be his best bet.
He has to make Robinson understand:

"What I need is more than a great player.
I need a man that will take abuse and insults.
They'll taunt you, goad you, try anything
to provoke a race riot in the ballpark."

Robinson looks like an earthquake about to happen.
"You want a ballplayer," he asks, "who's afraid to fight
    back?"
"I want a ballplayer with guts enough *not* to fight back.
A man who'll carry the flag for his whole race.
One incident could set us back twenty years."

Branch Rickey stares at Jackie Robinson
who stares at him, his eyes unsure, angry.
The office is silent, two men breathing,
the hum of traffic on Montague Street below.
Rickey knows this man must do what no one's done.
Is that too much to ask of any man?
"Mr. Rickey," he hears him say at last,
"I promise you there'll be no incident."

    1962

It was all such a long time ago.
Rickey's 81 and some days he feels older.
He has to grin at the tributes in the papers,
the politicians having their say now
when it doesn't matter much, not the way it used to,
the Governor, Richard Nixon, President Kennedy.

Dr. Martin Luther King Jr. calls Robinson
a pilgrim who walked the lonesome byways,
a freedom rider before freedom rides.
At least somebody finally got it right.
Hmm, wonder if he'd still call me Mr. Rickey.

Wouldn't miss it for new legs. Well, maybe new legs.
But Rickey's there in Cooperstown on Monday, July 23rd
for the final shining moment in that distant dream
as Jack Roosevelt Robinson enters the Hall of Fame.
It's been a while since reporters bothered with Branch.
Well, that's fine. He's had his moments in the news.
He finds a seat in one of two thousand chairs
set out on Main Street before the wooden platform
where the induction ceremony will take place.
He feels as anonymous as any fan, forgotten by many,
but then Jackie Robinson is thanking him,
saying, "Mr. Rickey was like a father to me."

Isn't that something now? And there's more.
Jackie plucks him from the crowd to tour the wall
where Jackie's picture hangs, like the other greats,
the white ones, all of them side by side in bronze.
As cameras flash around them, Jackie slows his pace
so they can make this final walk together,
old campaigners recovered from a bitter war.
Branch halts at Jackie's plaque and stares.
Nowhere does it mention the colour of his skin.

BEAUTY AND TRUTH

> "Beauty is truth, truth beauty,—that is all
> Ye know on earth, and all ye need to know."
> —John Keats

Tell that to the man whose wife
stands at an upper window, her eyes
wide and shining, ebony bangs brushed
away from her forehead, the skin beneath
that he loves to stroke, like alabaster
about to bloom, as if from the warm
touch of the morning sun, the curve
of her neck with the grace of a statue

as she bends to the glass, gazing down,
her nostrils flared, lips slightly parted
and just now beginning to tremble,
the hijacked plane five stories below,
the tower about to fall, her husband
even now on the phone, frantic to know.

WILF PERREAULT'S "VINTAGE LIGHTS," 2007

Except for the lights at the end of the alley,
the dim glitter of a backyard Christmas tree,
everything here is the blue of winter and evening,
the ancient Volkswagen huddled alone in a drift,
garages and sheds, blue snow drooping from roofs,
bare trees and poles a bleaker blue, the ruts
in the alley that lead past the boy
who can't be seen in the shadows,
the boy who is me, trying to be brave,
trying not to cry though he's pinned
by a knee on each of his biceps,
the bully above him burning
his cheeks with snow, the smell
on the bully of gasoline so strong
he fears they'll burst into flame
as he violently twists his head
and chafes to be free, knowing
the lights down the alley
are just about to go out.

152

REMEMBRANCE
for James Hiram Mondy

I never met my Uncle Hiram. He died
in 1917, two decades before my birth.

Every November 11th I think of all the time he lost,
his two younger sisters living well into the '90s,

his older sister surviving him by 77 years.
My aunts kept his photo on the wall,

often said I'd look like him some day.
And for a few years I guess I did,

but Uncle Hiram stayed twenty years old,
his smile as calm as a perfect day in spring,

his body buried somewhere off in France,
a graveyard no kin of his has ever seen.

I can't fathom what he faced over there:
trenches, barbed wire, screaming shells,

and Vimy not a part of history yet,
but just a ridge that needed taking.

What I think about is Mr. Merryweather
saddling his horse in the Paynton livery stable,

the ride to Grandpa's farm six miles west of town,
Grandma and the two girls still at home hearing

hoofbeats, stepping together into the bare front yard,
clutching at one another then, their eyes fixed

on Mr. Merryweather, the fingers of his right hand
clenched around the telegram.

THE DAYS RUN AWAY
(2015)

SATURDAY NIGHT

The bar is packed, the waitress too busy
running out orders, the table next to ours
filling with empties where two guys in suits
are arguing about how long on a hot day
it takes cement to set and how often
you ought to wet down a new driveway.
Two guys in suits. One of them—the one
with the tie like molten lava—says
he'd do it like this, and he sprays beer
on the pants of the guy in the charcoal suit.
That guy immediately stands up, wobbling a bit,
and kicks him in the shin. Then they begin to swing,
the table beside them bouncing each time they miss
and knock against it, empties clicking like castanets.
At a side table a big mother in a leather jacket
is bumped by one of the lurching suits, his girl
telling him he can wipe the floor with both at once.
He throws back his chair, curling his hands
into sledgehammer fists. Now here's a little guy
wearing a T-shirt that says, "Mother Mary
comes to me." He grabs two bottles
from the table that's jammed with empties,
tosses one into the air, picks up another,
lofts it too, then the other, three beer bottles
spirally over his head, he's juggling the empties,
his eyes focused ten inches in front of him,
hands flashing out, catching and throwing,
the rhythm of an athlete at his routine.

The guy in the leather jacket picks up his chair
from the floor and sits down on it, grinning,
caught in a spell of whirling bottles.
The fighters in suits turn to the juggler
whose bottles flash three feet over his head
until he gradually lowers the loop, bringing them down,
catching them one by one in front of his chest.
Everybody in the bar busts out clapping and cheering,
the charcoal suit offers to buy the juggler a beer,
"Yeah," says the guy with the lava tie, "and I'm paying."

BETTER THAN DETENTION

They've hardly listened to her
since the second week of September
and she thinks of her Methods prof
who loved to say, "Every teacher's job
would be so much easier if she were allowed
to shoot one student her first semester
—understand, we're not talking murder here,
just a flesh wound, say somewhere
south of the crotch."

She wants gags for the eight girls
who never stop yapping, basketballs
to bounce off the heads of boys who stare
at the clock, a trapeze to swing her
over miscreants, so she's silently
suddenly there, a ruler's whack
to the back of the head, or music, eh,
jack up the volume, give the rappers a taste
of Perry Como and "Bibbidi-Bobbidi-Boo,"
fill their ears till they're comatose, and catapults
rigged to every desk, the launching buttons
in her upper drawer. Better yet,
crazy glue in their chewing gum,
land mines in their lunch bags,
                              or maybe
she needs
              a change of career.
Yeah,

go back to singing lead with "The Wild Bunch."
Lord knows, she's got the pipes for it now.

THIS TIME

They're talking at the breakfast table
before their son goes off to school.
Three bowls of cereal in front of them.
"Lumpy porridge again," the husband says.
His wife slams a cup down in front of him,
sloshing coffee, three drops hitting his lap.
"Sorry," she says, "but you complain too much.
"You need to get out of the house, get a job."
But he has another month of pogie left.
He'll put her in her place. "That's real nice,"
he says, "coming from the stay-at-home mama
who hasn't worked herself in eight years."
She hesitates, scrubs at a stain on the coffee pot.
"Hasn't worked, eh? Who cooks your meals,
smart guy? While you lay around on your butt
and watch the stupid television day and night."
He looks down at his hands, his palms callused,
scars on his fingers, the tip of his thumb missing.
"Well, yeah, and who worked eighty hours a week
all summer long to keep you living high on the hog?"
"That would be the lazy slob who hasn't once
lifted a finger since he got back home."
She's glaring at him, her eyes wet.
"You can take your smart mouth,"
he says, "and shove it up your ass."
It sounds stupid, but he doesn't know
what else to say. He sees her glance at their son,
and go back to polishing the coffee pot.

It shines in her hand like Aladdin's lamp.
He turns away, hears her start to cry.
Then he sees their son getting up, retreating
from the table. His quivering lower lip.
Backpack for school beside the door,
he passes it by, hurries outside. Turns
to look at them. This time he isn't crying.
He slowly shakes his head and raises his arms.
Bends his knees like a boy about to spring
from a diving board, straightens
his legs, and he begins to rise,
no flapping of the arms, but somehow
he's gathering speed, going up
and up, a wisp of cloud around his shoulders,
and he's just a dot way off in the heavens.
The wife right beside her husband now, looking up,
both of them hushed beneath the empty sky.

THE GIRL FROM MAIDSTONE

Her father invented an oil furnace
that worked so well no one believed it,
and now, waning away in a hospital bed,
he'd never find the needed investors.
For weeks the girl stayed with her aunt in the city,
coming home after visiting hours, a sleepwalker
slowly reverting to wakefulness, the college boy
who lived in the basement watching the way
she drew the house around her like a shawl,
the shape of her shoulders filling his mind.
Sometimes, bundled for winter, he walked
beside her across the icy bridge to the hospital,
her father's smile thin as the tube in his arm.
After a week the boy asked for a date and took her
away from the hospital's antiseptic air,
up the long stairs to the Capitol Theatre,
the giant screen that gave them somewhere to look
while their hands discovered each other. They floated
before the screen that was so much smaller
than dreams, his right arm around her shoulder
as she leaned into him, their chests heaving,
inhaling the warm air that took off the chill
from the old theatre, snow melting outside,
ice on the bridge to the hospital gone, the river
beginning to flow, Canada geese flying north,
their cries drawing her father from bed
to the window that was clear of frost
and warm to his touch as he stood

for the last time and gazed across the city
toward the theatre on Second Avenue
where he knew his daughter was falling in love.

HAMID

The boy who kneels on the dry hillside,
selecting small stones, arranging them
in a neat pile on a square of cloth that's been cut
from an old and worn-out burka, knows nothing
of article 104 of the Islamic Penal Code of Iran.
He knows only what his father has told him.
"Choose with care," his father warned,
a sharp stone in the palm of his hand.
"No bigger than this. Exactly the right size
for the infliction of pain. Never so big as to kill
—not immediately. This is important, my son."

The boy pauses, a sudden wind swirling
a spiral of dust around him. He digs
at his eyes as he has done again
and again this hot spring morning.
When he judges his pile large enough,
when he knows the time has come to leave,
he lifts the four corners of the cloth,
knots them tightly together, rises, slinging
the bundle over his shoulder. He takes
another cloth and rubs at his eyes, needing
them dry for those below who might notice.

Walking slowly down the hillside, slowly
picking his way between boulders,
he approaches the sheltered spot where,
surrounded by the men of the village
and buried carefully up to her breasts,
he will find his favourite sister.

THE DAYS RUN AWAY LIKE WILD HORSES
OVER THE HILLS
(from a title by Charles Bukowski)

The weeks gallop from summer into September,
gallop away from the lake, a sheen of ice by the shore.

Hoofbeats hammer the gulch where deer hide from the hunter,
echo across a dry slough; a last goose cries in the empty sky.

The weeks snort at a sliver of moon, shiver in the night
of the coyote, its chill call stretching across the land.

Snow obscures the moon, now frost-bitten, withered,
and piles into gullies and hollows deep in the hills.

The nights grow long; the weeks grow shaggy and lean.
They lunge and plough through drifts that plug the valley.

Where the wind whips the hillside almost bare,
they paw at the snow, their jaws tearing the grass.

Winter lodges among them, the frozen carcass of winter,
and spring, next spring, will it ever come?

Bunched together in the lee of a thicket,
the wild horses neigh and neigh and neigh.

CARRIED AWAY

Hendon, the prairie village where my mother groused
at the wood stove while I squirmed at the kitchen table,
all the good pictures done in my colouring book.
I needed to go to school. "Next year," she said,
"when we move at last to the city."
Would we have a car then, I wondered,
a Ford, maybe, to ride us away to a lake, a river,
a city park with monkey bars and a paddling pool?
When my mother tucked me in for the night
she drew her chair close to my bed, her voice
hardly a whisper as she told of the skyhorse
that would land by my window, its giant wings
settling and folding, its saddle glazed by moonglow
and empty, till my foot hit the stirrup and I hoisted
myself onto his back, his wings lifting,
and we rose over the village, the prairie
stretching farther than I'd ever seen, dark
shelterbelts and sloughs gleaming with moonlight,
scattered farm houses, kerosene lamps in their windows.
Stars surrounding us, I gripped the reins, his mane
in my face and the cool night air, his shoulders heaving,
wings rising and plunging as I fell slowly
to sleep. Anything could happen now.
I knew somehow we'd get away. The next day
I climbed to the kitchen counter, stretched
for the mason jar on the top shelf, reached
and had it. Took what I was daily forbidden to touch.
I walked away from the village, started the fire

that spread, fanned by giant wings, smoke
rolling, wind driving the flames back toward Hendon.

MATINEE

"It was really nothing at all," the manager said,
his voice calm as our living room couch,
but when Gene Autry strummed his guitar
the whole screen crackled with static,
something wrong with the pot belly stove,
the bunk house filling with smoke,
the kids in the front row beginning to cough
though Gene kept singing, the cowboys
grinning and joining in on the chorus
till someone yelled, "Fire!" and everyone
fought to get to the aisle, the kid behind
clawing to get by me and I must have
elbowed him in the gut, almost falling
when he gave me a shove and I slipped
on something spilled on the floor, but I
jammed myself into the aisle, kids
wedged shoulder to shoulder, pain
in my heel, someone trying to climb
over me, but I wouldn't go down, I grabbed
for the big kid in front, got his belt and hung on,
the two of us upright, driving through the mob,
noise all around, yelling, screaming, someone
stepping again and again on my heels,
and then the lobby, there was room
to move, and we pushed through the door
and outside—fresh air—we sucked it in and
I looked down at my sore heel and the shoe
on my left foot was gone, the kids still

shoving, some of them crying, the manager
telling us to settle down, it was nothing
really, we should let our parents know
it was only a little smoke, the manager
standing firm in his sock feet.

UNDER THE BLANKET

Our fathers were singing in the front seat,
driving back to town for a block of ice,
our mothers in the shack at the lake,
frying chicken on the wood stove,
patting the sweat from their faces
with homemade cotton aprons.
The two of us rode in the back seat,
an Indian blanket over our heads,
you a year older than I, both of us
giggling, waiting for the next bump
to bounce us together. You leaned
toward me, breath stroking my right ear,
and whispered, "Now's your chance.
Do you want to see?" I did
and I didn't. Unable to speak,
I nodded my head and waited
in the snug world of the blanket.
I saw your lips twist into kind of a smile
before we lowered our heads and looked down:
your brown thighs tanned from days at the beach,
your hands tugged at your shorts, your panties,
sliding them down, a mound untouched by sunlight,
and in the smooth white flesh directly below
an improbable groove that stopped my breath
and altered forever the gait of my heart.
We must have reached the ice-house then.
When I came up from under the blanket
the first thing I saw was my father
handing me a chip of ice in a cracked cup.

I remember the slippery feel of it,
cold and hard on my tongue,
and how quickly it melted away.

CAUGHT

The older boy shows him exactly
how to set a snare on a rabbit trail.
Next day he takes five feet of copper wire
from his father's basement workbench,
folds it into his loose leaf binder,
takes it to school. No branches here
to pin to the ground, he wraps the wire
around the steel leg of his desk,
loops it into a noose, twists a slipknot,
sets the noose upright in the aisle.

The teacher checking arithmetic books,
moves ever closer down the row,
pauses at Kenny's desk in front of him.
sidesteps slowly backward, the noose
slipping over her shoe, tightening,
the twist of wire tearing her stocking.

When, hands shaking, he finally gets her free,
she points to the cloakroom door,
lifts from the centre drawer of her desk
the strap, thick black leather. "For you,"
she says and follows him out of sight.
He lifts his hand at last. Strives to hold it still.

"You like to play games so much, try this."
She raises the strap, slams it hard
four times against the far wall. Frowns.
"You behave yourself," she says "or else
the class will learn what happened here."

LONG WEEKEND COMING

Half an hour with my thumb in the air,
night dropping down, rain clouds looming,
and I swear it's hell being young and broke.
A red Corvette roars past, the bugger, tires
squealing, but wait, he's braking, backing up.

I slide in and we're off, leaving
the speed limit far behind, summer
a blur with the windows down,
his ducktail in flight, a rush
of wind and radio music, both of us
singing along, growling the blues.
He leans over once and tells me
he's got a big date in Regina tonight,
"How about you, kid?" and all I can say is
"I'm going home, home for the weekend."

Chamberlain is where he'll drop me. He slows
for the town, spots a Maccam Transport semi
already around the corner, picking up speed on #2.
"Hold on," my driver says. "Let's get you a ride."
He crushes the gas pedal, takes the corner
on flaming tires, the car leaning, leaping ahead,
a minute more, we're beside the semi
and past it, my driver waving his arm,
waving him over, the trucker's head
at the window, a puzzled scowl.
My guy vaults from his car, hollers,
"This kid needs a ride to Moose Jaw."

By the time I climb up to the truck, he's scorched
a turn into the asphalt and he's off for his date.
The trucker sits with his hand on the shift.
"That one of the boss's sons?" he asks.
"Maybe, yeah, it must've been." He nods, shoves
it into low. "They're used to getting their way."
I settle in for the ride home. Forty minutes later
he lets me out at Maccam's, and I walk into town.

Night air sweet as the lilacs on Main Street,
the moon shines through a canopy of elms,
my steps buoyant, music wafting toward me,
a sprawl and sparkle of lights down the hill,
and I see it's a street dance, a live band
on the sidewalk, couples waltzing on pavement,
a cluster of pretty girls huddled together, swaying
in their summer dresses, feet tapping, they wait
for the guys to get up their nerve—I'm walking
faster now, I can see their smiles from here.

IN THE DARK

I've just settled down with the evening paper
when the doorbell rings. Someone collecting
for cancer, I think, or maybe a kid on a bottle drive,
but it's a colleague from school, the music teacher,
his voice shaking as if he's expecting disaster.
"Yours was the closest place I could think of,"
he says. "I need a drink. Bad."

I can see that he does. He's pale
as a full moon in the morning.
He watches me pour him a rye, waves
me off when I reach for the mix.
He seizes the glass from my hand,
takes a quick swallow. And another.

I point to a chair, but he shakes his head.
Looks around the kitchen as if he wonders
where he is. How he got here.
"What is it, Terry? What's going on?"
He tells me about a boy from his band,
the kid who's so good on the sax, eighteen
years old. Working on the farm. Damned
tractor, he rolled it, was pinned underneath.
Gone before anyone could get to him.

Terry says he thought he'd pay his respects.
Went to the family home. His eyes
flick away from me. Out the window.

"Horrible, the grief," he says. "You can't
imagine how bad it was. I couldn't handle it."
He glances down at the glass that hangs
in his right hand. Lifts it, swallows
the last of the rye. Wipes a drop
from his chin with the back of his hand.
When I offer another, he backs away.
"No," he says. "Better get home while I can."

I walk him to the door and watch him go.
His car on the street, front wheel on the sidewalk.
He gets in, interior light waning as he cranks the ignition.
The car starts, but it doesn't move, engine idling,
loose bumper vibrating a bit at the back.
He's just a shadow in the dark car.
I see the blaze of a match, the flame
raised to the cigarette in his mouth,
the ember flaring and fading,
darkness all around.

210 HIGH STREET EAST

We were young and spry, taking
the stairs two at a time to Lorne's place,

just a couple of rooms really, the top floor
of a wartime house, Lorne the first of us

with a place of his own, where we partied
into the early hours, where all of us came

after the bashes that needed retelling,
reliving; after the weekend at Buffalo Pound

when the waves rose and slopped
over the sides of the rowboat until

the lake poured in and the boat went under.
Four of us clutching two paddles, free arms

scouring the water, we felt our toes touch
and lose the submerged boat that bobbed below,

prayed it wouldn't go all the way down.
We glared at the shore and shouted for help

till Bentz awoke in the shade of a pine
and galloped madly from cottage to cottage,

finally finding a man with a boat who bounced
over the waves to give us a lecture.

Back in Lorne's place we needed to talk,
oh man, how close we'd come to cashing it in,

nodding our heads, the whole gang perched
on his couch or sprawled on the floor,

beginning to believe once more we might be
immortal, we'd last as long as this house

whose walls could never contain our laughter,
and you might argue about what fools we were,

for some of us now are gone and two of us live
in the seniors' high-rise, on the exact spot

where that old house was razed, broken
shingles and boards carted off to the dump.

HE VISITS ALONE

Back from the States, fists clenched,
he sits on our settee. He looks
lonely and small, elbows jammed
onto his ribs as if he's holding
his heart inside. When we ask
about his wife, he says tonight
it was best to leave her at home.

His face impassive as a stone hammer,
his breath like a rap beat while we wait.

He leans back, seems to relax,
his eyes suddenly well with tears.
"It's ALS," he says, "Lou Gehrig's Disease."
My wife gets to him first, hugs him.
I wrap my arms around him too,
his frame already smaller.

Later, Kleenex stuffed back in our pockets,
he describes their visit to the family doctor.
"Seemed like all he could talk about
was how I was going to die. How bad
it would be. She didn't need to hear that."

BY AND BY, LORD, BY AND BY

I

A deep breath. Ready now, he settles on the lift,
touches the button, and is carried up the stairs,
a circle of friends, his poetry group assembled.
No need for his walker here, he rises, steps
into the living room, right toe dragging.
Before anyone can move, he's down,
flat, his face aflame. "'s okay," he says
as they help him up, "'s okay!" as they
lower him onto a straight-backed chair.
"'s do poems," he says, his face still flushed,
and they begin, copies of the poems circulated.
When his turn comes, someone lifts the poems
from his file and sends them round the room.
"Bob read," he says, and Bob reads his poem
which everyone discusses in the old way.
As if this were just another meeting.

II

When the poets have gone, he rides
the lift back to the landing, takes another
down to the basement, a full body sling
hanging from the ceiling, the sling
his wife will have to use any night now,
the only way to lift him into bed.
A wheelchair sits in the corner of the room
A hospital bed is waiting too, beside
their own double bed. She helps him
wriggle out of his clothes. Into pyjamas.
He falls back and she lifts his legs
onto the mattress. Lying down at last.

By his right hand the bell he taps for help.
Near his shoulder the bi-pap machine,
the mask that clamps over mouth and nose.
When his lungs won't work fast enough.
When he can't gasp sufficient air, chest
heaving, eyes wide and rolling white,
the flesh raw on the bridge of his nose.
Once he inhaled poetry like oxygen,
but it's not enough, no metaphor
can fill his lungs.

AT WORK

Mounted on a shelf beside your bed,
Joyce's *Ulysses*, your prized boxed edition,

richly illustrated, but here
above your chest, nothing but black letters

on a white field, an alphabet board,
letters in five stark rows, the rest of the board

blank as concrete that's smoothed and set,
lacking even the scrawled initials of a child.

Each row begins with a vowel. I point
at the first row, hoping to help you

revise a poem. No reaction. The next row.
Nothing. On the third row you force

your eyelids shut. Yes, it's one of these: i, j, k,
l, m, or n. On the fifth letter you squeeze out

another blink, and you've begun to choose
a better word, one letter, one arduous letter

at a time, labouring on a lengthy poem
that parallels an esoteric work by Bach,

its structure precise, thirty-two parts, each aria,
each canon, complemented by a sonnet, the result:

"Variations on Glenn Gould's Goldberg Variations."
Your eyes follow my slowly moving finger

over the dark letters, while mine stray
from the creases in your sweating brow

to *Ulysses* displayed here like the world's last book,
and I remember that James Joyce, almost blind,

wrote in red crayon letters on huge sheets of paper,
neither of you willing to surrender

before the final word is done.

ULYSSES

The book he was always planning
to finish, that beautiful boxed edition
mounted on a tripod, displayed on a shelf
across the room from his library wall,
the thousands of books he's already read,
thoughtful lines highlighted, certain poems
marked with ticks in the table of contents,
I could see that book tossed in the river,
the long winter's ice broken at last,
floes grating against one another, stripping
rushes and brush from the banks,
ice jammed at the turn, piled high,
water rising, rising, slabs of ice driven
over other slabs of ice, some thrust
above the banks, sliding across the road
or ramming trees, tearing them loose from shore.
Downstream the footbridge at the golf course
is battered, it convulses, collapses, is carried away.
Amidst the grinding ice, the sound like mourners
beginning to wail, his book caught in the current
is hammered this way and that, its box like a boat
barely keeping afloat in the surge, it takes on water,
is squashed between giant wedges of ice, breaks
loose and bobs along on the torrent, the box cover
torn, peeling away, it eludes a falling tree, sinking
low, is swept past a floating bench, around a tangle
of brush on the curve and out of sight, gone
in the April flood, but what I see is the book

plucked from the river, in his hands and open now,
he turns the pages surely, his eyes tracking the story.

ONE-WAY TICKET
(2018)

THE CHILDREN'S GAME

We played the game on Sundays
when my parents turned up the volume,
engrossed by Mr. DeMille and his Lux Radio Theatre.
Our playing field was the bare basement below,
the coal bin in the far corner, furnace beside it.
My friends and I put cardboard boxes
over our heads and shoulders,
switched off the single bulb
on a basement beam, lowered our heads
and charged one another, rebounded,
bumped something or someone, knocked
something else, slammed into concrete walls,
bounced off the furnace—its pipes quaked and rattled.

At the top of the stairs a sudden light as the door
swung open, the looming shadow of my father.
"You boys, keep it quiet down there. You hear me?"
We waited, breathless and still, for darkness to drop,
then crept away from the furnace and began again.
In the other end of the basement, we attacked, flung
ourselves into the darkness, lunged at every sound,
pounded and battered each other till finally we fell,
panting and spent on the concrete, sweat
on our heaving chests, not understanding why
we so desperately wished the girls from school
could be with us here on the floor.

EVERYTHING WE KNEW

When Kenny and I were twelve we knew everything
about sex. We'd studied the word "friction"
in our *Highroads to Learning School Dictionary*:
"the action of one object rubbing against another,"
and we knew what that meant. We'd seen Rita
Hayworth do the Dance of the Seven Veils in *Salome*,
her body whirling and swaying before King Herod
as the veils dropped away, one delicious veil
after the other, her bosom moving toward us, smooth
and round, so different from the shapes of the girls
at school, who always blushed in health class
and stared down at their desks. Sometimes
Kenny and I would talk in our backyard pup tent
about doing it, about exactly how you would do it,
we'd discuss what it would mean to be in the same bed
as Rita Hayworth without any clothes on.
We were horny and hard in our sleeping bags,
yearning for Rita and her twin sister to join us.
We knew even then we could do something about it
—friction would do the trick—but we understood
the dangers involved: pimples and hair loss,
brain fevers, blindness, and bent peckers.
So we clenched our fists on our chests, wishing
for girls to marry, free at last to give it a try.
But what about girls, we wondered, why
would they put up with it when there was
nothing in it for them?

GODSEND

Danny led me into his parents' bedroom,
both of us on tiptoes though no one was home.
He slid open the top drawer of the dresser
and when he lifted out a pile of sweaters
I caught the faintest whiff of lavender,
the same scent I once smelled mixed with
cinnamon when Mrs. Elliott leaned close
to hand me a sticky bun warm off the counter.

"You won't believe what I found," Danny whispered
as he folded back a plaid skirt and lifted it out,
a foam rubber breast, round
as half a grapefruit, an upright nub
like a real nipple in its exact centre.
I thought of Mrs. Elliott in her purple sweater,
the way her breasts pushed out the cloth.
"You know what?" Danny said. "It's called
a falsie. If you want, you can hold it a sec."

I reached and took it, the nipple's nub
like a living thing in the palm of my hand.
A rattle at the back door. I stuffed
the breast under the skirt, Danny hurling
sweaters into the drawer shoving it shut
and we flung ourselves down the hall
floorboards bouncing and howling back
to his room our breath hammered the wall.

Chest heaving, heart pounding,
I collapsed against the closed door.
I wondered if he'd ever show me
the second falsie. But did it matter?
I already knew exactly how
it would feel in my other hand.

After that I never once looked at Mrs. Elliott
without thinking she must be a bit of a phony.
She was a great mother, always
giving us cookies and stuff—why would she
want to look like a movie star in a sweater?
A week later, I overheard my own mother
whisper to my father that Esther Elliott
was beating the big C, she'd only needed
the one surgery, and that was a godsend.
What was the big C, I wondered,
and what the heck was a godsend?

HEAVY HITTER

What was it like to be Masayuki Yamakami,
my Japanese friend from grade three through twelve?
In the war years he and his whole family
were interned somewhere out past the airport,

though none of us kids knew about that. Later they moved
into town, his father starting a dry-cleaning shop on River
      Street,
his sisters practicing piano, becoming so good
every soloist in town wanted to work with them,

and Mas—or Sam as we called him then
in our nicknaming days—could slam a soft ball
so hard it would fly so high over the outfield
it would land on the roof of King Edward School.

Sam passed through town once in the '90s.
Checking messages, I heard his name, his voice
on our answering machine; going through
to Winnipeg, sorry to miss you, was all that he said.

But there he was in his Central Celtics jacket
for our 50th anniversary class reunion,
Sam, immediately recognizable as himself,
the happiest, youngest-looking guy in the group.

And by then I had some idea of how his family
had been carted off from their homes in B.C.,
their lands and boats seized, everything
they owned taken away, loyal Canadians

labelled enemy aliens, and how did he do it,
my old school friend, who somehow managed
to be the most popular kid in our class
while his classmates collected war comics

and dreamed of killing Nazis and Japs?

HIS PRESENCE

As important as your own bank account,
he said to me, every boy should have one.
My father's jackknife with the worn blade,
the one he used for years at the office,
sharpening pencils to a point as precise
as the figures he wrote in his ledger,
I kept it for years in my sweater pocket,
the sweater I wore for warmth in the archives,
sharpening my own pencils, their points
carefully carved in memory of him.

Often while writing at the long table
my hand dropped of its own accord
into that pocket, my fingers wrapping
around that pearl handle, solid,
like my father's grip on my shoulder
when he thought I'd need cheering.

My sweater draped over a chairback
while I walked outside in the heat of noon,
I returned to the archives and dipped my hand
into the pocket. Found it empty. Nothing
but a bit of lint in one corner.

My father suddenly as distant
as a hill on the far horizon,
a lone coyote howling
at a fading moon.

SAVING THE FISH

I lean over the river, water sluggish in summer,
a sunlit shimmer that shows me a boy, skinny,
his bomber jacket too big for his shoulders.
He's bent over with a pail in his hands, scooping
up fish where the ice is broken, where water
slides between rocks at the shallow spot,
some of the rocks laid there by the boy
to make a stable crossing into the woods,

the rocks like a dam then, frantic fish gasping
and flopping, beating themselves on the rocks,
the boy with the pail of fish lugging them
downstream to where he's chopped a hole
in the ice, his driven task to deliver the fish,
release them into deeper water, then run
back to scoop up as many more as he can,
his pants crusted with ice,
the boy out of breath, legs shaking
from the strain of running, but refusing
to pause, carrying pail after pail,

the boy who must've been me, and what relation
is he to the man leaning over the water a moment,
then slowly turning to shuffle along the paved walk
by this same river, the man shuffling
because his left knee is stitched with pain
when he hurries, the man having forgotten
till now that boy desperate to save all the fish
which the man knows were nothing but suckers.

WHAT HE WANTS

His body knows what he wants.
Not the girl from his sixteenth winter
who sat beside him in chemistry class,
and stared at the test tubes he filled,
never raising her eyes to his face.
Not the girl he proposed to
the year after college, the girl who said
yes, then went off to Australia,
writing her marvellous letters
till one said she wouldn't be back.
Not the woman he married, the woman
who loved him and stayed
till the children were gone.

His body knows what he needs.
One last walk through the old house
where he lived with his parents:
the kitchen where he dried the dishes
his father washed, while his mother
picked out tunes on the next-room piano;
the bare basement with the plywood sheet
balanced on saw horses where finally
he beat his father at ping-pong;
the dining room table where they gathered
together at the warped crokinole board,
wooden discs flicked from flashing fingers;
the narrow hall with the homemade bookcase,
bottom shelf jammed with Hardy Boys mysteries
and Walter Farley's Black Stallion books;

and at the end of the hall, his own room,
the desk where he copied Will James' horses,
and the bed with the quilt where he slept at ease
till the wake-up call of his mother's soft voice, the bed
where even now his body might sleep through the night.

ANOTHER MORNING AFTER

His mind burning with the idea
he can't quite grasp—something
he stalked moments ago
in a dream, a cougar padding silently
through shadows, but gone into the woods
each time he raised his rifle, or was he
the beast fleeing a man with a gun?

He steps out of the shabby bedroom,
rumpled pants draped on the chair behind him,
socks and shorts by his shoes on the floor,
empty bottle of scotch beside them.
Yawning, rubbing the bruise on his hip,
he walks through the rented house,
his eyes closing each time he yawns.
He stands naked in the open veranda,
shivering, his bad knee beginning to ache.

In the east the sky is already bright,
a line above the dark hills as red,
he knows, as the whites of his eyes.
Another morning on its way, one day
after another till it's over, and never
a sign that anything matters at all.
His mouth dry as the fluff under the bed,
he stares and stares at the morning sky,
astounded once more he's glad to be here.

FREE BREAKFAST AT THE COMFORT INN

The room crowded, tables small, my parents at one,
my older brother and I at another, I saw the woman

at the next table slide the scarlet nail of her index finger
under the skin of the mandarin and begin to strip

the peel away from the lush orange pulp below.
My brother, the teenager, glanced at our parents

and stopped eating his muffin, which, without looking,
he set on his styrofoam plate, his eyes on the woman

with the scarlet fingernails, that one nail moving
steadily under the skin of the orange which fell

away, revealing more bright flesh,
the orange cupped, round and fresh, in her palm.

She tore off one section, her nail
piercing the flesh, a sudden spurt of juice,

and she took that piece of orange on her tongue
and drew it slowly into her mouth, my brother

sliding the paper napkin from the table
and dropping it onto the lap of his jeans.

I was young then, watching my brother,
and wondered why I was blushing.

609 MAIN SOUTH

The meals in a black bag packed in styrofoam,
you cart them out to the car, place the meals-on-wheels card
on the dash, check the delivery list, and there it is,
the address you'll never forget, your family home,
where you lived from grade three to grade twelve
and the year you worked saving money for college.
You deliver the other meals, keep this one for last.

From the car, you see a garage in the backyard
where Nipper's doghouse stood, the lawn
where you staggered walking tall
on homemade wooden stilts, vinyl siding
covering the stucco you helped your father paint.
You climb the steps where you posed in your first suit
the day you graduated from high school.
You ring the buzzer at the front doorway
you haven't entered in thirty-one years.

A Chinese man opens the door, ushers you in.
Shuffling backwards, he motions to a small table
in the entryway. "Just put it here," he says.
Hands shaking, you extract his main course,
his soup and dessert, place them on the table.
"When I was a kid," you say, "I used to live here."
His eyes are on his meal, but he nods, says,
"Uh huh. Been here fourteen years myself."

You lean into the living room, bare hardwood,
not an area rug in sight, nor the sofa on whose back

you rested your elbows gazing out the window,
watching the snow fall and cover the street
where you and your friends played road hockey.
All the old furniture is gone, of course,
as are your parents, an abyss opening
inside, and you realize, oh Lord,
how much you still miss them.

THE LAST READING

She remembers when first they asked her
to give the reading at church her hands shook.
The thought of standing before the congregation,
all those people in the pews, everyone staring at her.
How would she ever manage it?
Her legs would quake, her voice falter,
she'd probably drop the Bible on the floor.

"You can do it," Joe said. "We'll practice at home."
Her good husband getting her to stand and read
while he sat before her, a congregation of one,
telling her she was doing fine, but she could
slow it down here, raise her voice there for effect.
She read the passage from Genesis again and again.
Read it at last in church, scripture flowing through her
like the Jordan River sweeping off to the sea.
After that, whenever she was asked to read,
she rehearsed with Joe, her confidence growing.

Today she fears her voice will waver,
but she'll do the reading anyway, will do it
for Joe, who's with her here in church.
She steadies herself, takes a deep breath,
catches the scent of fresh roses,
the pastel arrangement on the coffin lid.
A deep breath, and she does it for him.

DEPARTURES

By now I should be expert at farewells
but life balks and rears, then gallops away

from goodbye. Colin shakes his head
when he sees me enter his room, a package

of brownies in my hand. No appetite,
he says, and we talk baseball instead.

Benton tells me it won't be long now
before he's back home; the next time

I visit there's a stranger in his bed.
Lorne and I strain to lift a makeshift porch roof

above his outside door. It will not fit.
Joan is feeling tired when we drop in,

her eyes drifting shut on casual chatter.
Flash and I laugh together, the old days

back again, polished bright as morning.
No way to know we're done, they

slip away without a chance to share
what I could only hope to say.

With Gary it's different. My hand
rubbing his left knee, "I love you, buddy,"

words that catch and collapse in my throat.
We both know that this is goodbye.

THE ONLY TICKET YOU'RE GIVEN

The ticket sewn into a patch on your jeans
like the name tag stitched under the collar
of an old man's shirt in the nursing home,
—you'd never know it's there, life heaped on your plate,
a meal you want to devour again and again.

The days ahead rush at you, greyhounds
after a mechanical rabbit, always a winner
to cheer for, the race on now and always,
you could run it yourself, your limbs
working like oiled pistons, but you discover
the ticket concealed in your jeans:
there might be an easier way.

Night falls, and you count on the new day,
as sure of it as of Sunday's roast beef dinner
—till your best friend drops at the office,
his heart stopped, change like a Freightliner truck
descending a hill, brakes failing, a curve ahead,
you at the bus stop just around the corner.
You've got that ticket you'd rather not use,
but departure might be safer than staying,
a crowd pushing to board, and why does
the ticket feel like cement in your pocket?

The driver says, Hold on, buddy,
this is a one-way ticket, you might
want to get off, but he's laughing at you,

shaking his head as the doors slam shut,
the bus rolling forward, and there isn't even
a seat at the back. You sway in the aisle,
wobbling with each bump and jerk, fighting
for balance, desperate to stay upright, dark
tunnel gaping ahead, the road narrow
and heaving, pavement broken.

NEW POEMS

NEW POEMS

AT THE CLYDE BEATTY CIRCUS

Mom and I sat in the stands, four rows up,
an aisle below and right beside us
a wire-covered tunnel that ran toward
a large cage, and near it seven clowns
crammed themselves into a tiny car.
I laughed and laughed as the last clown
jammed shut the passenger door,
his giant butt hanging out the window.

The roar of a frenzied beast rocked me
and I looked down, a hungry lion
right there, wanting to eat me,
his mane wild, his eyes wilder,
teeth huge and yellow, a cord of drool
flipping as he swung his massive head.
Flimsy strands of wire between us.
He roared again, his mouth wide,
a mouth that could tear off my leg
and swallow it in one gulp.

I crouched against my mom, her arm
falling tight around my shoulder,
but what could she do?
The wooden row where we sat
shook and wobbled, the lion
rearing, his shoulder shoved
against my seat, the wire
about to break, other beasts
behind him, raging to get at me,

a bang then, like a rifle blast,
but it was a whip, a man with a whip,
the lion running toward the cage,
the other cats behind him, the man
cracking his whip, making them
jump through hoops and pose
on wooden boxes,
                    and the next time
I played in the backyard with my dog,
Nipper, I'd snap and snap
a towel, I'd train him to growl
and bare his teeth,   just wait
until the neighbour's cat
or any cat came near.

THE OLD BALL GAME

A warm night in July, my father and I
in the grandstand, our guys
in the field, their man on first
when the batter slapped a grounder.
It was a close play at second,
the base runner lunging into the shortstop
who was flung upside down and fell
on his face, hard, dropping the ball.
The fans three rows in front of us
were on their feet, fists in air, yelling:
"Dirty player!" "Throw the bugger out."
"Hell, yes, get rid of the coon!"

Puzzled, I turned to my father.
"What's he mean—coon?"
My father looked down at me,
pausing a moment, brow wrinkled,
his eyes fixed on mine. "Coon," he said,
"that's a word ignorant white guys
sometimes use for black men.
A bad word.   An insult.   Something
you and I would never say."

I have no memory of who won the game
or who the opposition was,
but even now, twenty-three years
after my father's death, I can recall
that moment, ball players standing

jaw to jaw, the stands in an uproar,
and my quiet father leaning over me,
his hand squeezing my shoulder.
Never—in all the years he was alive—
had I seen him look more serious.

MY UNCLE

My uncle, the farmer,
hated the farm. Riding
a tractor, sowing a crop,
there was never anyone
to talk to. He preferred
the beer parlour, a table
of friends, glasses rising
and falling, warm laughter
and talk that went up
and around and doubled
back again, supper waiting
at home in the oven, drying
out, and what did he care?
He wouldn't be here
to play Crazy Eights
with my aunt and me.

I remember the smell
of beer on his breath,
the way he took a quick
sideways step sometimes
when coming home late.
Also the times he talked
about baseball though
I never saw him play.
He said that farming
had ruined his back.
He was the umpire

for town games, bent
behind the catcher, legs
splayed, calling strikes
with a snarl. He never
played catch with me.
Couldn't do it, he said.
It hurt to throw.

Sometimes after a game
both teams would pile
into their cars and head
across the tracks and
into the bush, my aunt
and I driving home alone.
Once, in the morning
after a game, I awoke
and found a ball glove,
a three-finger model,
on the side of my bed.
My uncle said someone
from the visiting team
had too many beers and
left it behind. There was
no way to reach him, I
might as well have it.
My aunt shook her head.

Rich red leather, pliable,
a pocket that fit my fist.
I spent the morning outside,
tossing the ball as high as I could,
running like mad to catch it.
At lunch with the glove
on my lap, I examined the strap,
its underside with letters scratched
in the leather, J.M., letters
I traced with my finger.
My uncle's initials.

WATCHING THE COWBOYS

We loved Saturday afternoons at the Royal Theatre, popcorn
boxes flying, sunflower seeds as thick as dried manure
under our feet, whistles and catcalls whenever a cowboy
took off his hat and kissed the rancher's daughter.
Oh man, those movie cowboys, even their names
were magic—Roy Rogers, Gene Autry, Johnny Mack Brown,
Wild Bill Elliott, the Cisco Kid, John Wayne, Hopalong
    Cassidy.
We loved the way they leapt from galloping horses,
knocked bandits from saddles, spilled them
down the hillside, a rolling frenzy of flying fists.
Loved the way they slugged it out in saloon brawls,
chairs and tables flying, bottles smashed, mirrors broken,
the good guys giving and taking magnificent punches,
their white hats never disturbed on their heads.
Loved the way they handled their six-guns,
drawing and fanning the hammers to fire,
enemy weapons shot clean out of their hands.
                    Best of all
was the Durango Kid after the outlaws,
a flying leap from the saloon roof to the back
of his horse at the hitching post, the horse
gone in a cloud of dust, the outlaws doomed.

Donnie said he could do that, and Saturday after the show
we rode our bikes to his farm south of town, watched
him untie his Shetland pony, lead it to the barn door,
then climb to the loft where he paused,

staring down, the look on his face not a bit
like that of Durango or Roy, but we urged him on
till he jumped, landing spreadeagled, the pony
exploded away, farting, but already Donnie
lay in the dust, writhing, clutching
his crotch, though we knew his jewels
were jammed like meatballs deep in his throat.
Watching him, we were hardly able to walk.

The very next Saturday we saw Lash LaRue
face a masked man with a gun, a crack
of the whip, the gun torn from his hand,
but something had changed, we wondered now
if any of this had ever been real.

REAL WORK

The summer after grade ten my dad got me my first real job,
at McCargars' Feed Lot, west of town, and I could hardly wait
to tell my friends I had work as a hired man. I toiled
from 8 am to 6 pm with an hour off for lunch
which meant a full meal, and if I was lucky a slice
of Meg McCargar's peach pie, then a half hour of freedom
while my older workmate, the boss's son, caught some sleep
and I read *The Saturday Evening Post*, Norman Rockwell's
     paintings
so different from my job: a boy and his grandpa heading
for the fishing hole, girls flirting with a soda jerk, and me
without a driver's license trucking hay to the north field,
forking it out to the cattle, or twisting the posthole auger,
sweat blurring my glasses, hands sore beneath my gloves,
hole after hole, replacing posts in the fence by the hay bales,
or forcing cattle into the shoot, a needle jabbed into their
     haunches
while I attacked those with horns, sliding a two-by-four
over their necks to hold them, then straining at the
     dehorning tool, horns
lopped off, steers bawling, rolling white eyes, sometimes a
     spray of blood.

A sore muscle day that dragged on forever, until I caught
a ride back to town, the boss's son dropping me off at the
     corner
before he met his buddies at the bar, and I was home at last.
Water running in the clawfoot tub, I set the radio on the floor

and plugged it in, stripped off my work clothes, and sank
into the water, hot as I could stand it, full of suds, lying there,
muscles relaxed, aches easing, submerged for at least half an
    hour,
immersed in warmth and sound, just lazing, floating on the
    melodies,
pitchfork and posthole auger, wretched cattle fading like steam
off the bathroom mirror, song after song on the radio, me
    beginning
to sing along, belting it out with the Crew Cuts, the Four Aces,
even Tony Bennett, and I figured "Sh-boom" was right,
life was hard, sure, but it could still be a dream.

REX ROOMS

1956, and I'm fresh out of high school,
the pharmacy apprentice at the Moose Jaw Drug,
corner of River and Main, River the street of ill repute.
A block and a half away is the Rex Rooms
where the pool hall guys say hookers are selling sex.

Once when the delivery boy is off work sick,
the boss fills a prescription and asks
if I'd mind walking it down the street.
I check the address: #3, 159 River Street West.
A sudden apprehension: it'll be the Rex Rooms.

Will there be a pimp waiting, switchblade in hand?
I drag along, slower and slower, till I'm there.
The building is dirty red brick, a narrow
wooden doorway, dark windows above.

I knock on the door and wait. Wait some more.
Give them time to get out of bed, I think.
Let them pull on some clothes. Another knock,
still no answer. I push the door open. A shadowy
hallway. Not a pimp in sight. Nor a hooker either.

I stand listening. No springs squeaking.
Closed doors down the hall. Numbers over the doors.
I tiptoe along, looking for #3. Floorboards shudder and shake
like my own quaking knees. I pause at the door, fist
raised, ready to knock. No moans, no heavy breathing.

My hand has hardly touched the door,
when a voice calls, "Come in. Come in."
An older man, Chinese, face pale and lined,
a worn bathrobe over corduroy pants, he sits
in a still rocking chair beside the bed,
its blankets stretched taut as elastic.

I pass him the prescription, count out
change for the twenty he gives me,
and get out of there fast. I've been inside
the Rex Rooms. But no sign at all of a hooker,
and nothing to tell the guys after work.
Do I dare say there was a woman down the hall
—nearly naked—trying to lure me into her room?

STOLEN NIGHT

The old dream is back again
scratching at the window screen,
wanting in, and Lorne is there on the sofa,
the girl beside him in bathing suit and overcoat,
but the other girl, the one who's with me,
is down there alone, and I'm floating
up here, the living room ceiling
dissolved in a mist, but through the haze
I can see the girl walk to the record player
where she tears open a pizza box
and pulls an album out. What I want
is a song by Elvis Presley, the one
she needs to hear, "Don't Be Cruel,"
but somehow I know it'll be Dean Martin
singing "Memories Are Made of This."
Wait! She isn't going to play a song,
she takes the stylus and scrapes the needle
again and again over the record, Lorne shakes
his head and lights a candle, dribbling hot wax
on the rug, a pattern like the trail of a snake.
There's a sound at the front door, someone
coming, and for sure it's going to be my parents.
I know I can still fix everything, but there's no ladder,
no way to get down, and I can tell I'm lighter,
drifting higher and higher, the living room
falling farther away, as small now
as an empty cigarette box, and Lord,
don't let them know I've been smoking.

LETTER TO MR. FROST

They claimed you were paid over two thousand dollars
to come here and read us your poems. Boomer,
beside me, said for that price we could afford a movie star,
Charlton Heston, maybe, or at least Tony Curtis, not
some old goat guaranteed to bore us to death.
When you started to read, Boomer looked at me
and crossed his eyes, then slumped down in his seat.
I was surprised how much your words moved me.
The auditorium was hushed, twelve hundred students
waiting for each line that gripped and held us.
Poem after poem, your words filled the room
with images, heaving ground and boulders spilled
from a stone wall, a neighbour returning a stone
to the wall, looking like a savage armed for battle.
Your voice was low and gruff, almost a monotone,
but it carried every word out from the lectern
and into our ears. Boomer leaned into me.
"Where in Hell do you suppose they got this guy?"
He shook his head and slumped even lower.
It looked as if he might slide onto the floor.
That was when you stopped reading, everyone
waiting to see how the poem would end,
but you were looking in our direction.
Your voice suddenly loud, you were shouting.
"Sit up! Where were you raised?"
We all sat up. Boomer too. He looked like
a kid caught stealing in the Five and Dime.
I glanced around the auditorium.

Even our teachers were sitting up straight.
You hesitated then and said the poem
was ruined for you. You didn't finish it.
I'm not sure what you read after that.
It felt as though we were all caught in a balloon
that had ruptured, the rubber stuck on our faces.
When you finished reading, nobody said a word.
We couldn't wait to get out of that hall.
I decided then that I didn't much like you.
Yet lying in bed that night when I closed my eyes
I could see you stopped on a snow-covered trail,
way out in the woods near a frozen lake, snow
drifting down, your horse tugging at the reins,
the falling flakes and your rising breath—pale
shimmers of light on the longest night of the year.

IN THE LIBRARY

You're doing research in the reference room
when a young couple enter, both in blue jeans,
fake jewels on her pockets, holes in his knees.
She has four studs in one ear, five in the other.
You notice a drop of mucus on the guy's nose,
then realize it's a ring in his left nostril.

She asks the librarian at the desk if she can see
the obituaries for everyone named Spielman.
You watch the librarian disappear into the archives,
the guy pull out two chairs from the long table
next to yours. "Spielman, Schmielman," he says.
"What does it matter? You're a McGonigal now."

That's when you notice the rings, thin gold bands
on ring fingers, left hands. No engagement ring.
"Ancestors matter," she says. "They intrigue me.
I want to know exactly where I come from."
"I don't know about that," he says and laughs.
"An obit's just gonna show where you're headed."

She gives him a quick punch in the arm,
then glances at you, a blush colouring her cheeks.
You study the Encyclopedia of Saskatchewan,
Woodrow Lloyd and the Medicare crisis, 1962.
Put her in a crisis, you could swoop in, save her
from gutbucket boy with the ring in his nose.

She'd like that; she'd dissolve in your arms,
sweet as sunlight in springtime, warm and ready
for whatever you bring her, him quickly forgotten,
him with barbed wire tattoos like scars on his wrists.
When you look up again, the librarian has left them
three brown envelopes—that's all, just three obits.

She opens one, and delicately draws out
a browning newsprint clipping. She's all soft curves.
"Adeline Spielman," she says. "No relation of mine."
You watch him reach for the other envelopes,
open them, slide the clippings over to her.
She shakes her head, sighs, wanting your flesh on hers.

"Not much point to this, is there?" he says
and stares at you, his voice suddenly
loud and clear, "Hanging around here, eh,
snooping in other people's business."
You see that the doctors struck on July the first,
but what you feel is your face, consumed by flame.

BACK THEN

Chill evenings in the fall take me back,
the gang of kids that played hide and seek
in early darkness, kneeling by caragana hedges,
behind garbage cans and garden sheds, rushing
breathlessly for the street light on the corner,
yelling "Home free!" as our hands slapped the pole.
Night after night, we inhaled magic from the air
whether running soundlessly with sneakered feet on fire,
or wrenching carrots from neighbours' gardens,
raiding them with care and predetermined rules,
two carrots each, always from different rows.
Then we fled, our shadows lost in deeper shadows.

In grade eight the bigger kids were gone to high school
and we ruled the nighttime streets, walking arm in arm,
guys and girls together, we were the riders in the sky,
singing songs of the saddle, heading for the last round-up.
If anyone would falter, someone always knew the words,
saw the light, heard the lonesome whistle blow
as we strolled together on the Navajo trail,
the Colorado trail, the old Chisholm trail,
wandered through the Red River Valley,
walked the streets of Laredo, crossed the lone prairie,
under a Texas moon, yet never once left Moose Jaw.

We swore sometimes and acted tough as barbed wire,
swaggered a bit, showing off before the younger kids.
Surging with power, we always sang in harmony

and, fleet as colts, ran nighttime streets and seldom
touched the ground. We were all free to believe
in a day when anything might be, our arms
wrapped around the shoulders of our friends,
we somehow carried each other into a future
where nighttime streets were only pavement
and dusk just meant the end of day.

AVAILABLE ON iTUNES

On the computer, fiddling with iTunes,
I stumble across a group from the '50s,
The Gaylords—is that a name they'd use today?—
but there's that old song, "From the Vine
Came the Grape," and I'm a kid again,

the Zenith tube radio on top of the fridge,
CHAB in the morning, my father almost ready
for work, whistles along, his blue tie knotted,
my mother humming as the toast pops,
joins in: "from the vine came a dream to a lover,"
oatmeal porridge spooned into my bowl,
a layer of brown sugar melting through milk,
warm glow from the radio dial, sweet taste
in my mouth, my mother kisses my father goodbye,
strawberry jam on my toast, and in ten minutes

I rush out the back door, run down the alley,
cut across Coteau Street and through the hedge
to school, I'm there in plenty of time, my friends
shoot baskets and call me to join them. The bell
rings. Mr. Campbell strides through the boys' door
as we rush to line up, where once I got the strap
for disturbing the line by tossing my tuque
in the air, Dale and Kenny right there now
in front of me, daring to break the silence
telling knock-knock jokes that no one's heard.

Dale off these days with his second wife
travelling North America year-round in his RV,
and Kenny, the guy who worked CFL games for CBC,
Kenny gone now, deep in the earth forever.

THE VOLLEYBALL PLAYERS
(for Joel and Jesse)

What can I say for the boys who practice long hours
after school whenever the gym is free, the boys
who in one instant must dive to the floor, their hands

outstretched to save the ball from touching the hardwood,
and the next must leap above the net, hands raised
for the block that sends the ball slashing back?

I take note of knees that are scraped and bruised
and sometimes braced, of fingers fused together
with tape, of ankles swollen and bound with wrap,

and note as well the eagerness with which these boys
rush from the change room and into the gym, smiles
on their faces as they bump balls into the air.

What we do at your games is sit in the stands
and cheer. Dare I say something like this?
Our hearts reside in your heaving chests.

They spring with the ball off your straining hands.
They live in the air above the net, spin off
splayed fingers and bounce out of bounds, are smashed,

lifted, set and spiked, returned again and again
to the air. Our hearts are with you. They soar
when your legs hurl you weightless up for the block.

They sing again in our chests as they did
when we were young and immersed in games
that mattered more than math and physics.

We learn from you what we knew before:
to value the instant that lifts the heart and holds
us here in the marvellous moment that's now.

TWO TREES

> The trees around are for you ...
> —Wallace Stevens

An ordinary yard in the city, grass
neatly mown, shrubs and flowers
by the front step, but in the middle
of the lawn, a Lombardy poplar rises.
Three kids ride its branches,
waiting for our daughter to finish supper.
The dishes done, she joins them,
branches swaying with their laughter
as they talk about their teacher, his shirt
tail caught in his fly. They climb
high tonight, heaving themselves
into the upper branches.
People walking past may think
the tree's conversing with the wind
that stirs its branches, like a neighbour
leaning over a backyard fence to chat,
one who makes you glad to live in this town.

Their voices up above call me back
to the tall pine beside our rented cabin
at Emma Lake, the time I climbed so high
my mother warned me to come down
before I fell, but my hands were sticky
with sap—I knew I'd never slip—and I
looked down upon the faces of my parents
upturned and pale as white flags in the shade,

above them, weathered shingles mottled with moss,
then the row of tiny cabins leading to the beach,
and the lake gleaming in the morning sun,
a lone fisherman casting from an anchored boat,
his spoon flashing above the water
then disappearing with a tiny splash,
the lake as still as the branch
that held me so high
even now I can watch
the whole world turn below.

SLEEPING AND WAKING

When I was a child, my mother lulled me
to sleep with stories she made up

of the Skyhorse that would fly me
to a ranch on the moon. These nights

I read poems at bedtime, the day fading
behind flowing words. Sometimes

when I wake from a dream, I try
to slide back into the tide and ride

to a happy ending. Often now I sleep
like a pet cat until my bladder protests

in the middle of the night. When I return to bed,
my mind spins with the troubles at work.

"I won't be in today," said my absent co-worker.
"I'll call back later with an excuse."

When the house is quiet, no sound
but warm air churning through furnace pipes,

I like to recall the times that I read
"Winnie the Pooh" to my kids and how

children from a northern school wrote me once,
telling me they liked my peanut butter poem,

twenty-four letters packed into one envelope.
All her life my mother kept in the basement trunk

a copy of a short story she'd written, the story
rejected by a New York agent.

The day she received the news,
I wonder if she slept at all.

AUTHOR VISIT

Forty kids sprawled on the floor,
kindergarten to grade four, and I wonder
what the heck am I doing here?

Maybe I can seize them with my poem
that has a riddle for a title:
"What's smooth and brown
and on the bathroom plug?"

"Poop!" says one kid, a good answer,
but the poem is about a boy
who spills peanut butter

all over the house. One girl
likes the peanut butter
on the ceiling, another the father
who's an earthquake in pyjamas.

Laughter and smiles, the poem works,
my only poem for kids,
and there's still ten minutes to go,
three kids already rolling on the floor.

I've got a poem about a grandpa
who one morning tries riding a bike
when he doesn't know how.
It's worth a try.

"How about you—do any of you
have interesting grandpas?"
A flurry of hands. "My grandpa
buys me chocolate bars this big."
His hands as wide as his shoulders.

"My grandpa lets me stay up late."
"My grandpa lives in Moose Jaw."
They've been told it's my hometown.
Now a little girl waves her hand.
"My aunt lives in Nelson, B.C."

Another boy bouncing on the floor:
"My grandpa ..." but he dries up,
then blurts, "buys me chocolate bars
this big." His are a metre in length.

When there are no more hands in the air
when I've read my grandfather poem,
when we're done at last for the day,
a little girl in kindergarten raises her hand.
"Yes?" "Will you button up my sweater?"

After I tuck buttons through buttonholes,
she gives me a quick hug, and I marvel
at all that I've learned today.

GREETINGS

It's your birthday, somehow I sense it,
and I can't find the poetry book I want,
the Purdy Selected, cover photograph
of a scene deep in the woods, a tunnel
of light through the dark trees, and now
you're in the living room, waiting,
while I search through my book cases,
but nothing today's in alphabetical order,
some books shelved on their spines,
author names hidden, others falling
to the floor, pages flipped open,
a lone bookmark drifting down
like a yellow leaf in late October.

The book's a signed copy, the perfect gift
for you, and it isn't where it ought to be.
I start pulling books from the shelves,
checking title after title, stacking them
on the floor, one pile after another
growing higher, rising pillars of books,
there's a passage between them,
but they begin to shift, they're
collapsing on top of me, you still
waiting in the other room, but then
you're gone—and I'm in bed, sweating,
the bedroom cold, window open,
curtain lifting with a chill wind,
a car somewhere outside, the sound

of its motor diminishing with distance,
near silence then, a few dry leaves
skittering against the broken curb.

I turn over in bed, covers bind my legs,
I roll back again, thoughts churn through my head.
There's no way I'm getting back to sleep.
Might as well get up. Maybe I can find that book.

TIME MACHINE

Last night I dreamed of the boy I used to be,
out on the football field, promoted to running back,
awaiting the kickoff, his glasses off, the ball
a blur tumbling out of the autumn sun.
He waits and catches it, begins to run, cutting
left, then right, until he's hit, a tackler
at his knees driving him sideways, another
at his chest smashing him backwards, the ball
torn from his hands as he's crushed to the turf.
That, the beginning of his final high school game,
yet for years he sees himself as a football player.

He could never imagine this sedentary man
seated at a desk, a pen clasped in his hand
as he considers altering a word on the paper
before him, the page filled with leaves
shifting into shadow, and somewhere beyond,
the lazy lull of lake water, and here
beneath the underbrush, the bright
raspberries—he can feel his tongue stir
in his watering mouth, suddenly knows
that it's noon, three hours have surged by,
and, loving what he does, he's made
the morning disappear.

NIGHT ON THE PRAIRIE

A crescent moon like a splinter of ice,
its frigid light shining on miles and miles

of empty land. A dry dugout. A shallow lake,
its shoreline white with alkali. Stubble

sticking through a shroud of snow,
wind moaning in the dying shelter belt,

caragana bushes bent and broken.
A vacant house, front porch collapsing.

The barn behind it sagging into itself.
A ruined granary flatter than the stoneboat

that sinks into the earth by a pile of rocks.
Far along a gravel road, the only moving object,

a pickup truck swings around a curve,
headlights sweeping over pallid snow, bare fields

stretching to the endless horizon, dark houses
here and there, empty as the box of the truck.

CLOSING DOWN

Everything going for at least 50% off,
the department store closing down,
I come through the south door,
past the shoe department, and cut
through Ladies' Wear. "No bloody way,"
says a woman, her voice so loud
I stop to look, a tall woman in black slacks
and a red sweater, her back to me,
a clerk at the counter motionless,
a blouse suspended in one hand,
the other pointing at the neckline,
a guy beside the woman nodding
his head, a strand of grey hair
falling over his forehead. "No,"
she says, reaching out, her right hand
slapping him across the face, hard,
a whack like a cracking whip,
his left cheek flaring red, his mouth
hanging open, a dribble of spit
on his lower lip, the woman taut, almost
vibrating. The guy looks around,
sees the clerk watching, blushes,
embarrassed, but determined.
He takes one step toward the woman.
"Just what in hell," he says, "was that for?"
The woman stares at him, silently,
her shoulders hunched, a long minute
before she spins away, and I see

her lips clenched shut, her heels
striking the floor, the sound like shots.
The man looks at the clerk, then at me,
opens his mouth as though he might explain,
but then he shakes his head, and I think
I hear his teeth snap together. He shrugs
and follows her toward the door.

IN THE NEIGHBOURHOOD
   (after Jan Beatty)

The man next door says he doesn't talk to reporters,
says he doesn't know what to believe anyway, says
his neighbour was always a good guy, he'd cut
your grass when you were away on holidays.

The reporter points at the yellow tape by the door.
You must've seen traffic in and out, he says, strange
people coming and going at dusk, maybe. Heard noises
at night, eh, when the neighbourhood was quiet.

The woman from across the street says she knew,
always knew there was something wrong with the guy,
he'd say hello when you passed him in the street,
but he'd never look you in the eye, never pause to talk.

The woman with the pink apron shakes her head.
No, no, that was you, always in a rush, never time
to visit. He was a friendly guy. When I was down
with the flu, he brought me homemade chicken soup.

An act is all it was, says the woman from across the street,
your house so close to his, he needed you to approve,
couldn't have you suspicious, my God, four little boys
buried in his basement, their bodies dismembered.

The woman with the pink apron has tears in her eyes.
We don't know that. Everyone's spreading rumours.
He was a good man, a neighbour you could count on,
always had candies for my son ... oh ... oh, Lord!

MY FATHER NAMED HIM AFTER GORDIE HOWE

"You'll play hockey," he said. "Same as your brother."
By the time he was eight, Gordie could stick handle
just like Sidney Crosby and fire slap shots
like Boom Boom Geoffrion, that's what my father said.
I don't know who this Boom Boom was,
but I was only six and I knew for sure
that Gordie was already better than I'd ever be.
I tried, I really did, but my ankles were weak,
I spent more time wobbling and falling
than skating, landing on my elbows or my knees,
sometimes going over backwards on my head.
When I was eight and barely made the team,
my father said it really didn't matter, Gordie
was the guy in our family going places,
I might as well play soccer or broom ball,
or tiddlywinks, he didn't give a care.

Even after that, my father complained
if I didn't watch my brother play. Gordie
was good. And big too. He often scored
half his team's goals. Once, in a tournament
they beat Swift Current nine to one, and he
got eight goals. My father only yelled at him
twice that game. People said that Gordie
was a sure bet to make the NHL some day.
My father said you could count on it. He always
stood right beside the bench where he could grab
Gordie when he came off the ice and point out
any stupid mistakes he made.

My father had a voice that carried like a car horn.
When someone dumped the puck into the corner
you'd hear my father roar: "Get in there, Gordie. Now!
Don't be a bloody pansy. Knock him on his ass."
If Gordie was tired and resting up between shifts
my father would be yelling at the head coach
to get him on the ice before they lost the game.

My father always drove Gordie to tournaments.
It gave him the perfect chance to talk strategy
and contradict what he called all the dumb ass
advice his bloody coach had given him.
Gordie said he felt trapped on hockey trips.
Nothing to do but listen. The Old Man
wouldn't even let him use his smart phone.

A tournament in the next province, and Gordie
was slammed into the boards, our father
telling him to go after the guy, to break
his bloody face. Gordie snapped that night,
charging the other kid, fists driving, dropping him
to the ice, unconscious, Gordie gone to the penalty box.
After the long ride home, and the praise, all the praise,
Gordie quit hockey. He was just sixteen.
My father went nuts then, yelling at him,
yelling and yelling, all the money he'd spent
on fancy equipment and hockey trips, all of it
wasted on a no-good, ungrateful, lazy son
of a bitching kid who wouldn't listen to reason.
It made me thank the Lord for my weak ankles.

HOCKEY NIGHT

I like to remember the outdoor rink, boards
that kept the puck out of snow banks, prairie sky
full of stars almost as bright as the rink lights,
night air fresh and white with our breath,
pick-up games, and we all took a turn in goal.
Always we played till our feet were numb,

then made for the shack, roaring wood stove
surrounded by benches where we sprawled,
our feet thrust at the stove and beginning
to throb with life, our bones warming till the smell
of our socks drove us back to the ice.

Then the repeated thrills, breaking for goal, a pass
on your stick, the deke, the shot, puck in the net.
Transformed by ice and the night, Jari
Kurri and Paul Coffey beside me, I was
Wayne Gretzky veering behind the net.

I want to remember the way it was when sleep
would arrive as my head struck the pillow,
before my stomach was a burning knot,
my jaw sore, hands aching. A quarry of pain.

I try not to think of the game tonight, the moment
that always comes, when Coach says, "Come on,
big guy, time to earn your keep," when I throw
off my gloves and fight the other enforcer.

A GOOD TIME

I remember on Fridays you said
you'd rather eat at our place.
After supper we'd listen to 45s
in my basement room and sing along,
harmonies like the Beach Boys, my dad
saying we sounded as good as the Ink Spots,
whoever they were, nobody on the hit parade,
I guess, but you could go high and I
could go low, the kids at school
loved it when we got up the nerve
to do "Help Me, Rhonda" in the gym.

You said you never sang at home,
your old man liked his peace and quiet.
Your mother claimed when he was laid off
she could feel the tension in the house
like a cello string vibrating, smart people
knew when to walk on stocking feet.
You said you were smart enough,
you never had a shiner in your life.

When your old man was back at work,
you told me, he'd end the week
at the bar, getting hammered, then
stumble home with ragged nerves.
A good time to be somewhere else.
You said your mother knew how
to handle him, more or less.
Sometimes, she'd just walk away.

After high school you moved
to Toronto, chasing and chasing
a record deal. Signed a contract too,
a beauty of a girl singing with you,
Willa and the Wild One on the rise,
the papers said you were engaged.
"True Love Today," the song
you wrote, climbing the charts.

Clashes over what should come next, the perfect
song you'd need to follow up. Then they dropped
your contract, her picture in the paper, black
eyes and broken nose, I could hardly
believe it. Until I thought of your old man.
His long shadow. Like a finger snap,
the music world was through with you.
That I understood.

HER LETTER FROM SASKATOON

You left me for another woman,
left me in this house with its mortgage,
the traffic on 8th Street a constant moan
and irritation, the scramble of cars
past all those fast food joints. What
did I care about food? For a while
I thought I'll never eat again.

My heart was like Ford's Drug Store,
Mr. Ford so good to his customers
but dead now, the store's broken windows
boarded up, the building closed for years,
a guy on the corner trying to bum a smoke.

I spent hours on a bench in Kinsmen Park,
staring towards City Hospital, wondering
exactly what the doctors there knew
about suicide prevention, shrieks
and laughter from children riding
the animal carousel, the Ferris wheel
turning and turning above us.

Once a man sat on my bench, leather
jacket and haunted eyes. He began
to discuss the weather, the chance
of rain, his hope that the night might be
clear for the Perseids. I think he just
wanted to pick me up.

When the girls at work grew tired
of my moping around, they said, Enough!
It's time to celebrate. They claimed
none of them liked you. They all knew
you were a jerk. That night we went out
to the Bon Temps Cafe, wine and good food,
a toast to me, laughter and gossip, I found
that I could laugh too. And talk

to the man who strolled over
from three tables away. "Excuse me,"
he said, and I could tell he was weighing
each word as he spoke. "I haven't seen
you in years, but you must be Yvonne."

I knew him at once, of course, my guy
from grade twelve. He's a widower now,
going bald, but the smile that he gave me,
it's the same smile that used to melt
every bone in my body. I thought
you ought to know it still does.

THIS IS THE BOOK I BUY

A private eye with a smart mouth
claims his name is Doghouse Reilly
and after his client's hot pants daughter
sucks her thumb and falls into his arms
he tells the butler she's old enough,
it might be time she was weaned,

and the P.I. meets with the girl's father.
Seems the old boy's being blackmailed
and our guy is a straight shooter
though he doesn't carry a gun,
and he says, sure, he'll take the case,

he's thinking the daughter is as bright
as a burnt-out cigar, her head empty
as a panhandler's pockets,

but her older sister is smart enough,
with legs that run on forever, trouble
is, she loathes men like him and she's
already married three of them.

Later our guy does some tailing
and hunts around, finds the young one
seated in a high-backed chair, her legs
aren't so bad either, she's wearing
jade earrings and nothing else,

doped out of her mind, a camera
catching it all, and the photographer
dead on the floor, blackmail,
yes, and more going down,

and this is the book I give my wife
for her birthday, though we don't celebrate
much any more—let's face it, the kids
are grown and gone from the house,
and the evenings sometimes go on forever.

The lone streetlamp outside the window
has been burnt out for days, or maybe weeks—
who keeps track anyway?—and nobody,
not even the old woman three houses down,
comes by walking her dog, the whole street
as still and silent as dried blood on a carpet,

but a book quickens your breath in the dead of night
and no need for a bottle on the bedside table,
nor munchies and spilled crumbs on the sheets.

THE SINGER WITHOUT THE SONG

Carl only remembers a bit of what happened,
not the first night in hospital, body bruised,
limbs aching, tremors in his head,
a pool of blood on his brain, fog
rising in the dank swamp of his mind.
The fog that hangs heavy upon him,
that holds him for two months in bed,
unable to walk, no sense of taste or smell,
the music gone, every sound
just more pain throbbing in fog.

—

Hammered in the back of the head,
he was unconscious before he fell,
didn't see someone knee him,
smash his head into the concrete.
They punched him, kicked him where he lay.
His friend tried to hold them off, finally
fell on top of him, took the blows himself,
blood filling a crack in the sidewalk.

—

Carl was sorry he had to work that night, sorry
he was late for Eoin's bachelor party, the guys
whooping it up, paint-balling, drinking,
and Carl sober as a prayer, feeling out of it,

Saturday night, he'd rather be at home,
but he'd hang with the guys for a while.
When Eoin wanted to walk to O'Hanlon's,
Carl decided he'd better go along,
Eoin limping from an injury the week before,
leaning on him now, arm around his shoulder.

A bunch of guys about to pile into an SUV,
they stopped and stared, pointed, yelled:
"Hey, check it out. What have we got here?"
"A couple of queers." "Yeah, a pair of fags."
Eoin steadied himself, considered them,
tried to look sober. "Guys, we're just going by.
We don't want any trouble." The first blow
took Carl in the back of the head.

More than a concussion, a severe brain injury.
For months he wondered if he'd ever
recover, ever play and sing again.
Then the magic week when change began.
The fog lifting, he felt a stirring and a shift.

Now the music is back, the Library Voices
with a new album, seven of the songs
written by Carl Johnson who sings and plays
as if the music gods had just invented him.

THE LONG WINTER

At the edge of the park the dark rink, a ridge of snow
by the gate that is closed with a knot of twine,
no sign of a skater, the ground beyond obscured
by white mounds except where two men with shovels
have met and spliced together a trail through the trees,
stopping beside a single pine, its drooping branches
bent with ice from freezing rain. A thin squirrel crouches
on the branch of an elm, ice crystals
on its bark and thick in the air. Above it,
a few dead leaves cling and murmur
in the breeze, spreading rumours of spring
with the melt still months away.

Dogwood branches scratch at the boards of the rink.
Thatches of grass and twigs are squashed and tangled
where the shovelers have thrown their snow.
A lone woman slices straight through the park,
ignoring the path, her hand like a vice on the rope
of a sleigh that holds her groceries and child and
ploughs through the waves of snow, its prow bucking
the drifts like a yacht in a storm. Each step
she takes breaks the crust with a snap
and a crunch that launches her onward
until she pauses beneath the grey sky
and utters a loud sigh. She longs
for more than rumours of spring.

SHE NEVER SAYS

exactly what she's thinking
for fear the words might fall
from her mouth like confetti
on a wallflower at a wedding.

She paces the streets of the old town,
approaching the house where her mother
used to wait for her father's return.

She remembers his bedtime stories,
rich with exotic lands and sailing ships,
his fingers tracing patterns on the blanket
that was like a map of a world that is flat.

Should she stop now at the family home,
the broken sidewalk that leads to the porch?
An old man with a cane lives here.
She's seen him seated on the porch bench,
his stiff figure still as a piece of petrified wood.

He's here this evening, but his head is bent
as if he's asleep, and there's no reason
why he'd be the one to remember her father
or answer the questions she cannot ask.

If only the past would stay in the past.
Then she could deal with tomorrow.

TONIGHT AND TOO OFTEN

Again and again we laugh without joy,
thinks the man watching TV with his wife.
He cannot smile at the sitcom banter.
Too often he dwells on the news
—and the documentaries:

> the farmer, older than he is, plunging
> into the box of the grain truck where the boy,
> his grandson, has fallen, the two of them
> disappearing, drowned in a sea of wheat

> the sleeping baby wrapped in a blanket
> and laid quietly at night in a dumpster,
> the warehouse district in winter,
> where its cries echoed down into the silence

> Cree youngsters scooped up and away
> from their mothers, dropped into families
> whose skin shines like the nightlight
> in the bedroom just before it burns out

> the child who ran from the residential school,
> his home a hundred miles away, found
> curled beneath a fir tree, frozen solid,
> his parents never informed of his death

The man in front of the TV forces his mind
back to their daughter's wedding, her choice

of a husband the boy that they love, flowers
on each table from neighbours' gardens,
the banquet food assembled by friends,

and the glow of the couple as they danced,
the glow reflected on the faces of guests,
the smiles and the growing applause.
The world, he wonders, will it ever
resound with that kind of joy?

MY APOLOGIES TO YOU

I didn't do what I said I'd do,
and I'm really sorry it never got done.
Here's exactly what happened:
I was clipping my toenails over the toilet bowl
and pulled a muscle in my lower back;
I could barely crawl down the hall and climb into bed.

As a matter of fact, I hate vacant houses at night.
I'd rather masquerade as a piece of artificial turf
and let a dozen Rider receivers practice
making their cuts on my prone body. The truth is
I was on the sidelines, watching a Rider practice,
reaching for an overthrown ball, when a cornerback
cut me down with a slashing tackle. It was a quick trip
to the hospital, but eight hours in emergency,
nurses and doctors sniggering behind their masks.
I would've left on my own, but I couldn't walk.

Allergic to painkillers, I'm not an ideal patient.
I'm the gopher twitching outside his hole,
my tail torn off the time I was trapped,
and it's not growing back. I'm the kids' playhouse
in your backyard where feral cats gather to scratch
and scrap and screech through the night. I'm the frown
on your wife's face when she curses you
and the neighbour—that would be me—
you chose to check the house while you were gone.

Yes, I was the guy who forgot to check your basement,
the water heater failing again, the furnace room
wet, water sliding over your rumpus room rug,
rising, lifting the sofa, floating it against the wall,
busting the basement window, water pouring out,
a torrent in your backyard, a maelstrom of water,
and I'm awash with guilt, knowing it's my damned fault,
but the truth is I yearn for sleep and can't say I'm sorry
for your playhouse flooded with drowned cats.

THE DAY WE STOLE THE TRAIN

It's a bit like a dream, Dave Margoshes and I
walking beside the Pullman cars on this line
that hasn't seen a passenger train in years.
People gesture from the windows, complain
that they should have been gone an hour ago.
A porter stands in the doorway of the first car,
tells us the engineer must be asleep on the job.
Will this train ever get moving again?
Dave and I walk to the engine, a hiss
of steam by the tracks, but no sign
of an engineer or any other railroad man.
We climb into the cab and take control,
Dave checking the pressure gauges,
me grabbing a shovel and beginning
to feed the fire box, though there's no coal
in the tender, but thousands of crab apples
which are light and easy to fling. Pressure building,
the locomotive shudders ahead, the sound
of cars jerking down the line, Dave blasts
the whistle, and we pull away from the station,
picking up speed, passing a low-slung edifice
that must be a library, patrons looking up
from books and magazines, every one of them
flashing their thumbs up, and it's into
the countryside now, fields of canola
yellow as sunshine, a single blue field of flax,
and wheat flowing towards the horizon, Dave
and I leaning out the windows, wind cool

on our faces, a level crossing ahead,
a Mountie car with its lights flashing,
a man in red by the car, slashing his hand
up and down, but we're by him, rougher
country here, clumps of bush and rock,
rolling land that's never been ploughed,
and half a mile ahead the land drops away,
the rails running level and straight. We slow
the train to a stop, dismount from the engine
and walk toward a canyon with a river boiling below,
the tracks on a trestle of timber, old and weathered,
and we doubt if it can possibly carry a train.
That's when the Mounties arrive, four of them
flourishing handcuffs. Three surrounding Dave,
they pin him down and get the cuffs on his wrists,
the other guy grabbing me, but I shake him off
just as I'm shocked awake, and I worry,
will Dave ever get out of jail?

LIPTON, SASK. BALL TOURNAMENT, 1977

Here's how I remember that Fort San summer.
We writers cobbled together a team
—a money tournament—but we were in it for fun,
and what could be more fun than our first game?
David Carpenter at ease on the mound, tossing
pitches so slow no batter could wait for them,
slow grounders, easy bloopers to the outfield,
occasional strike-outs, our catcher,
Dennis Gruending, urging him on,
Hey buddy, buddy, pitch fire, buddy,
easy out, buddy, smoke him, buddy, buddy,
burn him, burn him, burn him,
his spiel a performance poem for the ages,
and we were putting them out, starting
to believe we could hit too and then
we actually scored some runs, Eli Mandel, our
coach, telling us he knew we could win this game.
And we did. Lost the next one, sure,
but who cared after our one, glorious win?

That night there was beer in the hall,
someone playing a piano, the whole team
gathered around, Robert Kroetsch singing,
"Cigarettes and Whiskey and Wild, Wild Women,"
then another song, and another, all of us
singing along, joy as pure as a double play,
the piano drunk and rocking, and that night
we leaned in and rode it, everyone of us,

we felt we could have stayed there forever,
but our throats grew weary, our voices hoarse,
the janitor saying how late it was,
he had to lock up the hall.

AFTER THE FREEZING

Country music in the headphones
drowns out some of the doctors' talk
but not the sawing nor the grinding.
Johnny Cash singing "Cry, Cry, Cry"
can't begin to cover the whack, whack
whack of the hammer, but I feel nothing.

That night I press the button on the cord
that's looped around the guard rail.
A bell rings slowly somewhere in the ward.
The incision on my right hip feels
as if a hot needle is stitching it up again.
The room is almost dark when Mary enters,
nodding when I request something for the pain.
She is big and black and competent, always
willing to answer the call. Beneath my back
I feel a bulge like a rope or a dead snake.
Mary lifts the shoulders I cannot lift myself,
smooths the wrinkle in the pad below.
When my urinal is full, I ring again.
Each time I thank her for dumping it,
Mary nods and says, "You're welcome."

Another day, Mary helps transfer me
from my wheel chair to the toilet seat.
I strain and manage what I'm meant to do,
then fold the toilet paper, reach for the grab bar
and lift my swollen hip, sweat on my forehead,
tremors in my legs as I clean myself.

When I'm composed again, the sweat
wiped away, my breathing calm, I yank the line
that rings a quicker bell down the hall.

The door opens, Mary leaning past me
to seize a wad of toilet paper. "It's okay,"
I say, "I'm done with that." Mary smiles
now, a smile that could set bells ringing
throughout a dozen wards, in distant village
halls and ancient church towers. It's possible
I'm beginning to fall in love.

FLASH

As sure as September follows August,
every autumn brings a card from you,
"Happy birthday, Mick!" Your love of puns
steadfast after all the years. Back in our college days,
we roomed together, you, riffing on Judy Garland's
old-time co-star, always called me Mickey Roomie.
We met playing high school football, you the linebacker
who scattered linemen and made your tackles matter,
and then at college you starred for the Hilltops, helped
make the team the nation's best. This while we stressed
and fretted over physics, our chairs back to back
at separate desks, until we finally swung around
to split the beer cooling in the window, and play a game
of crib, settling nerves so we could catch some sleep.
All the frigid mornings, cutting through Kinsmen Park
and walking together over the 25th Street Bridge, wind
sweeping along the frozen river, fingers numb
on briefcases full of books, then up the stairs
to the chem building, the coldest corner in the world,
but we did it, made it, again and again, passing
every class.
          And the summers, back home
working construction, even a job together
building Knowles Motel, shirts off, sweating in the sun,
and the evenings with the gang, hamburgers
late at Ike's Place, renting horses too for rides
through River Park, trips to the drive-in theatre,
two guys hidden in the trunk, easy evenings turning

into night as we lolled in your parents' living room,
shooting the bull or playing again and again Pat Boone,
his *Howdy* album, a bunch of us singing along,
that lucky old sun, rolling around heaven all day,
and that one night we all got drunk at your place,
you wanted us gone before your parents came home,
packed us into Clink's car to go to Ike's for burgers,
but you spun the wheel, drove instead south of town, flung
the doors open and told us all to damned well run it off,
a police car coming out of nowhere, lights flashing,
you upright beside the idling car, sober
as a power pole, the rest of us fleeing
across the prairie, half a dozen different directions,
the Mountie who caught you at the Grad party
shaking his head, "Oh no, not you again."

Then the summer of '60 I was best man at your wedding
and stumbled though a toast, nervous as a virgin in a cathouse,
and two years later you did a better job for me.
Decades in separate cities, separate provinces,
you in Winnipeg, a private practice dentist now, summer visits
meant good times around your backyard pool.
A whirl of years spinning past, and on your fiftieth anniversary,
my wife and I were there, and this time I gave the toast
and got it right, a tribute to my buddy and his high school
sweetheart who found a way to make love last.

My old buddy Gordon Keith, nicknamed Flash after a hero
from the comics, Flash Gordon, but the name fit the '50s
    linebacker

flying through a crush of blockers to snare the fleeing runner,
though not so much the widower now in the assisted living
    home,
shuffling down the hall to meals while leaning on your walker.
Ah, but there are visits to your room, that picture of your girl,
the same one that hung on our wall in college days, the one
she sent so you'd remember her, and here it is,
plus another of the old gang taken at your mother's funeral,
and we reminisce about the fits we must have given her,
and then there comes an email from your brother-in-law:
you were found deceased in your room, and it's all
over now, and no bloody way on earth to handle this.

AT FIRST I FORGET

Another morning and I've just finished
the stretches that help keep me moving.
8:00 a.m. and the phone rings, a number
I don't recognize, but by the third ring
I remember the day and pick up the phone.
"Well," says the familiar voice, "this is a big one."
My high school buddy from half the country away,
right on time with his annual good wishes.
The 21st of September, our shared birthday,
though he's a year younger than I, a mere 79,
using a cane now, he says, after a ball replacement
on his bad hip, the angle of the shaft out of whack,
like my back with its four failing discs
that make me ache when I stand too long,
but we remember friends who are gone
and will not settle on aches and pains.
We salute the new year like warriors
given at last a break from battle,
a table before us spread with food and drink.

WHERE I'VE LIVED MOST OF MY LIFE

I'm sitting on a bench on Main Street,
wind turning the corner by City Hall,
bringing with it chocolate bar wrappers,
a crushed styrofoam cup, a torn envelope,
crumpled sheets of newspaper, scraps
of our lives tossed on the street.
People hurrying by, their eyes half shut,
a whirlwind of dust rising around them,
I consider how long I might sit
before someone passes I'll recognize.

I used to delight in trivia games.
What band leader once sang backup
with the Hilltoppers? Billy Vaughn.
Who left his second best bed to his wife
when he died? William Shakespeare.
Who was on base when Bobby Thomson hit
the home run that won the '51 pennant?
Clint Hartung and Whitey Lockman.
With the slats of the bench grown hard
on my butt, a sudden thought blows in
on a swirl of wind: Who trusts memory anyway?

Thirty years I taught in this town.
I knew the name of every girl, every guy
in grade twelve, every last one of them.
When they came to my class, I put them
in a seating plan, warned them I was

watching them, but not to worry,
they hadn't sprouted warts on the nose,
I was matching names with their faces.
And where are those names today?

A woman swings out of the Pita Pit,
hair lifting over her collar. She walks
toward me, high heels rapping,
the start of a smile on her lips.
She looks like someone I may recognize,
but this is the moment the wind
hurls grit in my face. I close my eyes,
hear her footsteps fade and vanish.
Trust memory? At this moment I'm not
even sure why I'm waiting here in the wind.

TOGETHER AGAIN

Today, my old friend in the hospital
is confused and angry, seized by
hallucinations, afraid of drowning. After
the collision, its starboard side buckling, he sees
the great unsinkable ship fill with water and sink.

What we need here is a change of subject.
I tell him, when my granddaughter was young,
we placed pine nuts in the palm of her hand
and watched her eyes grow huge as loonies
while a chickadee hovered a foot from her face,
then dropped on her thumb to feed.

He continues staring at something I cannot see,
then looks at me, nods, and begins to speak.
He remembers his parents' yard, an oriole
at the feeder, feathers bright as mandarins,
flowers in the garden, and strawberries. He grins
and says hollyhocks in the fall, when stirred by wind,
would scratch at the wall like a witch's fingers.

RIDING HOME

You driving, me in the passenger seat,
long grass in the ditch bucks as we pass,
tires on rough pavement growling away
like Johnny Cash with a frog in his throat.
Back seat empty, no one to hear us,
we sing along with the radio, hanging
on a note, voices more than a little off key.

A fox darts onto the road, caught
in our lights, and you hit the brakes,
swerve as it skitters into the ditch.
Lucky for him, you say, I've still got my reflexes,
and you punch in another radio station, highway
like a big river curving ahead, the car a raft
on the wide Missouri taking us home, poetry meeting
over, we're done with poems for the night,
but your last one sings in my mind.

We're natural born music men, we've got rhythm,
we burn, burn, burn, oh, that ring of fire, the light
on the dash like the moon that a lone coyote howls at,
something more than noise released from within,
your fingers drumming the wheel, we bawl out the song,
and you say, Man, if we could really sing we'd probably
never have written a poem in our lives, not one.

A glow ahead above the horizon, it disappears
as the road drops into a ravine, but the city's just over the rise,

the city where you were born, yes, and the graveyard
where we'll bury you long after your driving days are done,
and I'll still be singing along with the radio, singing badly,
just me, wailing away and mourning for you.

SOMETIMES I THINK OF YOU DEAD

which is no surprise since you've been in the earth
for more than ten years now, thirteen years
since those falls that would prompt your wife
to phone and ask me to help you up and into bed.

Love is a seed that grew without water or heat,
it drew my wife and me to your side, week
after week, to help with the feeding, the massage of
wasted muscles, the reading of poems,

and how can I picture you dead when your mind
leapt from one project to the next, a writer's school,
a festival of words, a cultural centre, every project
brought to life by your drive and desire.

How can I possibly picture you dead when you marshalled
the rush of words that sprang alive from your mind,
when you made them dash and dart in poems so lively
they tore through the day and lit up the night?

Your projects and poems, they survive
and abide, they gleam with the flare
of your dreams in a day that would dawn
cold and grey without them.

    (In memory of Gary Hyland)

ADRIFT WHILE READING

What does he see this evening, a book heavy
in his hand, as he closes his eyes to doze?
A young guy in his father's '58 Ford, driving away
from Maidstone, away from the small town girl
he met in second year university, the only girl
who'd ever loved him, the one whose dark eyes
shone with magic when he held her, starlight
in her smile, and often a song on her lips,
a song he'll never hear again, it's over now,
it didn't work after all, too many miles
between them, they're done and
he knows it, he can't imagine how
he'll ever find another girl.

As the book slips from his hand
his eyes jolt open and what does he see?
A woman in an easy chair, a novel
open on her lap, the reading lamp shedding
light on its pages, the woman's eyes closed,
the shadow of the lampshade upon her,
a hint of a smile just visible, and he wonders
if she's recalling the luckiest day of his life,
the New Year's Eve he met her,
her resting face as beautiful now
after fifty-nine years of marriage
as it was then, the band swinging
into a tune that led them to dance,
a tune that sang of everything
that might ever be.

FINALE

There's silence on the beach at summer's end.
The teens who whooped and swatted volleyballs
across a single strand of twine are gone.
The boys who built the giant sandcastle
with a dozen towering turrets, the two girls
who delighted in pirouettes at the water's edge,
the woman whose beach umbrella heaved
and fell with every gust of wind, the man
who taught his son the deadman's float,
the brothers who fought over a single boogie board,
shoving, swearing, punching, until their mother
threatened to take them back to town
—all are departed. Gone too are the motor boats,
their skiers dropped off days ago, the boats
drawn onto trailers at the launch and trucked away.

What little wind there was died down an hour ago,
the waves lulled now, barely a whisper on the shore.
A lone gull walks the beach, bending now and then,
its beak snatching up a stray chip or sunflower seed.
Side by side on lawn chairs, an older couple sit,
gazing far across the empty sands, the vacant lake,
the sun sinking in evening haze, clouds and water
steeped in a dozen fading shades of red, the couple
silent and still as they await the coming dark.

THE WATCHER

Midnight, and there's a face at the window.
It catches the bedroom light only an instant,
then slides away, toward the backyard elm.
I can feel tightness in my throat
as I switch off the light and step
on shaking legs to the window.

Someone is out there.
I think I recognized the face,
deep-set eyes under a hooded brow,
but I may be wrong. Hope that I am.

Beneath the bare branches,
by the dark trunk of the elm
is a figure that shouldn't be there,
tall and enveloped in shadow, still
as a cairn on a burial mound.
Waiting. Just waiting. Until someone
decides what will happen next.

AFTERWORD
Robert Currie: An Appreciation
by Mark Abley

There's a poem in this book entitled "Turnip Butter." It comes from *Yarrow*, Bob Currie's second full-length collection. *Yarrow* looks back to rural life on the prairies in the 1930s; it's a rugged, plainspoken work of a kind that critics attuned to postmodernist theory might find easy to dismiss. I like it a lot. I particularly admire "Turnip Butter," a poem about hardship and hunger. More important, it's a poem about transformation:

> Then we sat around the table
> in the smoky tallow glow
> we peeled the turnips
> cut them into halves
> using kitchen knives we scraped
> and ate and called it butter
> butter sweet as California peaches
> We forgot the night the blizzard
> warm in the sweet glow of
> all our turnip suns

In defiance of winter and its darkness, Yarrow's family succeed in transforming the only food available—a jar of canned turnips—into bright pleasure. The poem ends with the glow of turnip suns, a vision of incongruous splendour, a note of quiet triumph.

This book includes a total of 161 poems, written over more than half a century. Rereading many of them, discovering others for the first time, I'm struck by their exactness and their candour. The violence endemic among boys and men— at the hockey rink, in school, on the farm, in the home—is a recurrent theme. Currie never shies away from describing precisely what he sees and feels. "This Poem Says What It Means" is the title of a single poem, but it could serve as a one-line summary of the entire book.

Currie records, he remembers, he reflects, but he seldom spins a web of images in the way that many other poets do. Indeed, he almost seems to distrust figures of speech. "No metaphor can fill his lungs," he declares in one of several beautiful poems about the illness and death of his friend and fellow poet Gary Hyland. "Beauty and Truth"—a rare sonnet, and one that comes with a Keatsian epigraph—could hardly be less Romantic: its subject is the 2001 attack on the World Trade Center in New York. This becomes clear only in the last three lines, just as an earlier poem, "That Day," leaves it until the final lines to demonstrate that the day in question is the one on which John F. Kennedy lost his life. The poem's impact grows not from speculation or overt lament but from the vivid everyday details of a man's life in a prairie town.

Miracles emerge on occasion—"the whole prairie a sudden radiance," Currie writes in an early poem. But those miracles don't come easily. They are likely to require the work of both nature and human imagination. In one of his loveliest phrases, he evokes "the scant calligraphy of willows." The writing is not on the wall but on the riverbank, and the adjective "scant" is apt for the dry terrain of southern Saskatchewan.

I realized, in contemplating these poems, how graceful and astute a craftsman Bob Currie can be. "Starting Out Together," for instance, relies on a subtle patterning of internal rhymes: "brake ... lake ... shaking ... quaking ... awake ... aching." Towards the end of the poem, assonance and rhyme flow together in a powerful stream: "pines ... park ... pain ... paw ... dark." This is a poem of love and deep foreboding, a poem vibrant with both hope and suffering. In art as in life, neither sensation cancels out the other.

Notice the length, or rather the brevity, of the words I've quoted from that poem. Is there a poet anywhere who makes less use of long words? If you think I'm exaggerating, look at Currie's late poem "At the Clyde Beatty Circus." Like so many of the pieces in this book, it evokes a memory or an imagining of childhood. There are forty lines in the poem, and just a single word ("passenger") is longer than two syllables. The effect is often blunt yet seldom abrupt.

In some of his finest poems, Currie begins with an apparently straightforward memory and turns it into something unexpected, almost magical. "The Summer I Worked Construction"—could there be a plainer title?—has an even plainer first line: "Two hundred and seventy-six miles from Moose Jaw ..." John Keats this is not: you won't find a nightingale or a Grecian urn anywhere in these pages. "The Summer I Worked Construction" is made up of a single sentence. But if you think the opening words suggest what Bob Currie is up to, think again. The poem soon moves into a touching evocation of love and personal loss, and it concludes like this:

> ... here I was, back on the pavement, driving
> through Paynton, the town I knew as a boy,
> the grain elevator where my uncle worked in the '40s
> burnished now by the sinking sun, no one knowing
> that one day it would fall, collapsing,
> a fury of splinters and dust, an expert
> imported from somewhere else
> to manage the blast.

From construction to destruction in a handful of decades and a mouthful of words: the impermanence of life is one of Currie's most persistent topics, and he comes at it in a host of unforeseen ways.

Not often does he write directly about art. There are more service stations than sculptures in this book. But I take his brilliant poem "In the Gallery" as a manifesto of sorts. It describes the feelings of a boy alone in front of Alex Colville's painting "Horse and Train." The boy's memory and imagination transform the work of art, just as he himself is transformed by what he sees:

> The boy is stunned, fixed, oil on canvas.
> Behind him his father appears at the door,
> calls his name, pauses, calls it again,
> the boy breathless before the painting.

"In the Gallery" too enacts a moment of quiet triumph, an act of gratitude. It is with boundless gratitude that I open and reopen the pages of this book.

NOTES

Yarrow was meant to be read like a novel, with individual poems telling the story of a prairie farm family in the 30s and '40s. The main characters are Jake and Agnes Yarrow, and their son, whom everyone simply calls Yarrow.

Klondike Fever is based on the adventures of Arthur A. Dietz, who in 1897 formed his own mining company in response to the discoveries of gold in the Klondike. News of the those discoveries so excited the world that one million people made plans to go to the Klondike and one hundred thousand actually put their plans into action. All over the world men left their jobs and headed for the Canadian north, many of them packing extra club bags, gunny sacks, crates—anything in which to bring home the gold they were certain lay waiting for them in creeks somewhere far to the north. *Klondike Fever* is an imaginative re-creation of the terrible journey of Arthur Dietz and the seventeen men who accompanied him on his expedition for gold.

The author hopes that selections from these two books may inspire readers to seek out the complete stories in the original volumes.

The first line of "What He Wants" is from Gary Hyland's "Body Song to Hypnos" in *The Work of Snow*.

"In the Neighbourhood" was inspired by Jan Beatty's poem "Stray."

ACKNOWLEDGEMENTS

Many thanks to those who first published my work in chapbooks: Delta Canada for *Quarterback #1,* Fiddlehead Poetry Books for *Sawdust and Dirt,* Sesame Press for *The Halls of Elsinore,* and Coteau Books for *Moving Out.*

Special thanks to the following book publishers: Oberon Press for giving me my big break and publishing *Diving into Fire, Yarrow,* and *Learning on the Job,* Hagios Press for *Witness* (as well as Radiant Press for permission to reprint poems from *Witness*), and Coteau Books for *Klondike Fever, Running in Darkness, The Days Run Away,* and *One-Way Ticket.*

Thanks to the editors of the following publications where some of the new poems previously appeared: *The Antigonish Review, Devour: Art and Lit Canada, Grain, Hearthbeat: Poems of Family and Hometown (Hidden Brook Press), Heartwood: Poems for the Love of Trees* (League of Canadian Poets), *Literature for the People, Numero Cinq, Saskatchewan Hockey: The Game of Our Lives* (MacIntyre Purcell Publishing), *The Society,* and *The Spadina Literary Review.*

For his invaluable assistance in preparing this manuscript, the author would like to thank his editor, Dave Margoshes. Thanks also to Lorna Crozier and Mark Abley for their generous contributions to this book. For much support and expert advice about poetry at various times over the years, special thanks to: Edna Alford, Liz Allen, Byrna Barclay, Fred

Cogswell, Lorna Crozier, Dilshad Engineer, Mary di Michele, Ted Dyck, Dennis Gruending, Gary Hyland, Judy Krause, Robert Kroetsch, Katherine Lawrence, Michael Macklem, Eli Mandel, Dave Margoshes, Don McKay, Jim McLean, Elizabeth Philips, Bruce Rice, Ralph Ring, Barbara Sapergia, Peter Stevens, Andy Suknaski, Anne Szumigalski, Geoffrey Ursell and Paul Wilson.

Additional thanks to Gwen Fisher and the staff of the Moose Jaw Public Library for their assistance and support. Also a tip of the hat to the staff and members of the Saskatchewan Writers' Guild whose support has been so important throughout the years.

Major thanks to JoAnn McCaig, Elizabeth Philips, and Caroline Walker of Thistledown Press for their faith in this book.

ROBERT CURRIE is a poet and fiction writer who lives in Moose Jaw, Saskatchewan, where he taught for thirty years at Central Collegiate, receiving the Joseph Duffy Memorial Award for excellence in teaching language arts. His books have been finalists for the (now defunct) Commonwealth Poetry Prize, the Acorn-Plantos People's Poetry Award, the Poetry, Fiction, and Book of the Year Awards at the Saskatchewan Book Awards, and the High Plains Book Award for Poetry. A series of his poems (later published in *Yarrow*) won third prize in the 1980 CBC Literary Competition.

A founding board member of the Saskatchewan Festival of Words and a former chairman of the Saskatchewan Writers' Guild, Currie once edited and published *Salt,* a little magazine of contemporary writing. Highlights of his career include receiving a Founder's Award from the Saskatchewan Writers' Guild, having a radio play win the 1977 Ohio State Award, teaching creative writing at the Saskatchewan School of the Arts in Fort San and the Sage Hill Writing Experience in Lumsden, delivering the Anne Szumigalski Memorial Lecture for the League of Canadian Poets, and serving two terms as Saskatchewan Poet Laureate. Currie is a recipient of the Saskatchewan Lieutenant Governor's Award for Lifetime Achievement in the Arts.